MW00439731

HEARTSTORMING

HEARTSTORMING

CREATING
A PLACE
GOD
CAN CALL
HOME

ROBERT J. WICKS

Paulist Press
New York / Mahwah, NJ

Cover image by Creative Travel Projects / Shutterstock.com
Cover and book design by Lynn Else

Library of Congress Cataloging-in-Publication Data
Names: Wicks, Robert J., author.
Title: Heartstorming : creating a place God can call home / Robert J. Wicks.
Description: New York / Mahwah, NJ : Paulist Press, 2020. | Summary: "Heartstorming provides a point of entry to the contemplative life for anyone who will become or remain open to the movements of God in their daily life"—Provided by publisher.
Identifiers: LCCN 2019036461 (print) | LCCN 2019036462 (ebook) | ISBN 9780809106639 (hardcover) | ISBN 9781587688997 (ebook)
Subjects: LCSH: Contemplation. | Spiritual life—Christianity. | Spirituality—Christianity.
Classification: LCC BV5091.C7 W53 2020 (print) | LCC BV5091.C7 (ebook) | DDC 248.3/4—dc23
LC record available at https://lccn.loc.gov/2019036461
LC ebook record available at https://lccn.loc.gov/2019036462

ISBN 978-0-8091-0663-9 (hardcover)
ISBN 978-1-58768-899-7 (e-book)

Published by Paulist Press
997 Macarthur Boulevard
Mahwah, New Jersey 07430
www.paulistpress.com

Printed and bound in the
United States of America

For the female and male vowed religious around the world who have truly sought to create a place God could call home. For me, this especially includes the following Sisters and Brothers, who are also long-standing friends:

Sisters Ellen Carr, OSF; Suzanne Delaney, IHM; Charlene Diorka, SSJ; Constance FitzGerald, OCD; Marie Gipprich, IHM; Loreto Hogge, RSM; Maribeth Howell, OP; Agnes Hughes, IHM; Barbara Jean LaRochester, OCD; Cathy Maguire, RSM; Maureen McGuire, DC; Rita J. Murphy, IHM; Joyce Rupp, OSM; Theresa Saetta, RSM; John Joseph Schuyler, IHM; Virginia Scirocco, IHM; Carol Tropiano, RSM; Kathleen Tuite, OP; Virginia Unsworth, SC; and Ann Raymond Welte, IHM. And Brothers Wayne Fitzpatrick, MM; Brendan Geary, FMS; Loughlan Sofield, ST; Kevin Stanton, FSC; and Kevin Strong, FSC.

Although this list may seem long, I have had a great deal of support in life. In fact, there are so many more women and men religious I should have included. Please forgive me for not mentioning you by name. I hope that you know you have also supported me and my ministry and that I am *very* grateful.

A Place God Can Call Home

When Jesus was born, he had a certain destiny
to make this world
a place God can call home.

As part of this journey
he called people to become
partners with him in its creation.

This meant helping all of us realize
that this world we live in is actually
the beachhead of the "kin-dom" of God.

Today, as we continue to experience this call
we may experience not only friendship and love
but also greed and hate at times.

We may encounter not only hope and open arms
but also those who would trade the joy of community
for the "security" of ME-first.

But still our smile never need completely disappear
nor the search to seek Jesus's goal
ever totally cease.

Because the desire for inner peace remains too great
and the love for community too powerful,
to stop seeking to create a place God can call home.

CONTENTS

CONTENTS

Part III: Creating Your Own Field Notes

PERMISSIONS AND ACKNOWLEDGMENTS

I would like to thank Oxford University Press for granting me permission to adapt material from my books *The Tao of Ordinariness*, *Night Call*, and *Perspective*.

I am grateful as well to Paulist Press and Ave Maria Press for publishing several of my earliest spirituality books, since they provided some of the material I was able to update, adapt, and share in this work.

Finally, as always, I wish to thank my wife, Michaele, for reviewing, editing, and reflecting on my words, ideas, and hopes to ensure that my message is best received by those I hope to serve in writing this book.

Introduction
COME SIT BY ME

An Invitation to Prayerfully Experience Living with More Meaning, Inner Peace, and Joy

When I was a young boy, I remember at times feeling a particularly intimate sense of closeness with God. Early on, it was due to experiences out in the rural areas of upstate New York. It also occurred when I was an altar server. For example, during the solemn high Masses at my parish in the neighborhood where I worshiped, the waft of incense would occasionally open me up to encounter the awe of God, especially during a beautiful Easter sunrise service. Even now as I look back, I can still remember one unexpected event at the parish that enabled me to touch the holy in a surprising way for me as a young man.

After serving at a daily Mass the week after Christmas, the pastor pulled me aside and asked if I were free on New Year's Eve to help out at a special parish social. In response I told him I'd just be staying home with my parents to watch the ball drop in Times Square on television, so I'd be glad to do what I could.

He then told me that a group of Catholic Lithuanian Americans had rented the hall beneath the church to celebrate New Year's Eve. At midnight, they also wanted to come upstairs to ring in the New Year at midnight with prayer. Since he would not be around, he asked if I would be willing to open the church, put on the lights, remain there until they came up from downstairs, were finished and left, so I could then close things down and safely lock up. The pastor, Msgr. John Balcunas, was such a gracious man that I was pleased to do this for him. Also, I thought it would be fun, and, as a youth, felt proud to be given such a responsible task.

At about 11:30 p.m., I went to the church, opened up, and turned on all the lights. I knew I really didn't need to do it that early but was afraid of being late and wanted to make sure everything was as perfect as I could make it. Finally, just before midnight, I put on my cassock and surplice, went out on the altar to kneel facing the tabernacle that was slightly elevated behind the altar, and waited for what was to occur—probably a few prayers would be said, guided by one of their leaders.

After a while, I could hear people shuffling into the pews behind me. I didn't dare turn around because I thought that would be disrespectful. Then just as it turned midnight, the organ sounded a note and the men and women behind me burst into song with deep, strong voices that mark the churches of Eastern Europe and the Eastern Rite. The powerful, rich timbre of their voices shook me. Looking back on this, I realize now it was an epiphany for me, a gracious opening to the sacred. These were people whose voices told of a vibrant love of and deep faith in God that the Sunday parishioners sometimes failed to communicate so well. Although at the time I didn't think of it this way, in retrospect it made me ask at some level: Why wasn't *my* faith like that? What would it take so I could have such a strong, dynamic Spirit within me?

Such awe of childhood doesn't last unless it is nurtured. Society, in general, has other goals in mind. As Rabbi Abraham Joshua Heschel cautions in his book *The Insecurity of Freedom*, "We prepare the pupil for employment, for holding a job. We do not teach him to be a person, how to resist conformity, how to grow inwardly....We teach children how to measure, how to weigh. We fail to teach them how to revere, how to sense wonder and awe. The sense of the sublime, the sign of inward greatness of the human soul and something which is potentially given to [us all] is now a rare gift."

Consequently, as time went on, the incense, New Year's Eve experience, and many other portals to experiencing the Divine in church, other people, and nature, were ignored, inadvertently blocked, or even—at times—consciously prevented. I did this by filling myself up with unnecessary needs, grasping, and egotistical pursuits, as well as becoming absorbed in minor and major habits and addictions that mark most people's lives in today's secular society. Yet, as we see in so many stories from the Hebrew Scriptures and the Christian New Testament, *God always pursues.*

The challenge and question that remains for us is this: Will we be open enough to see and embrace these sacred movements in our life when they cross our path? Furthermore, are we willing to set the stage to actively search for and welcome the Divine into the heart of our lives? In my own case, later in life, I was to respond to such questions more powerfully while teaching one summer at St. Michael's College in Vermont.

Each time I went to teach at "St. Mike's," I would have periods of silence and solitude that were longer than usual for me. Beyond the classes, daily liturgies, and meals, there were long stretches of "alone-time" (time in solitude or quietly being reflective) for the three weeks I was there. It also provided the time and setting for meditation, writing, taking long walks by Lake Champlain, or simply sitting in the sun outside the back door of the townhouse the college provided. All of this offered the opportunity to rest, renew, and open a space that greets God in ways my usual bustling, intense schedule involving helpers and caregivers always seems to defeat.

One of the specific results for which I was particularly grateful during these times away usually included receiving good insights into what I was studying and teaching. Also, interacting with the wonderfully committed students and the outstanding faculty I was privileged to teach alongside made me realize anew the importance of what in India they refer to as *satsang*, the company of good people. The entire time there was often so refreshing and enlightening.

Even though I failed in some instances to fully appreciate what my time there might offer, I consistently struggled to be as aware, grateful, and welcoming of the Spirit as I could. I did this by making as much space within to unlearn and encounter life in new ways so that touching the holy would truly be possible. I wanted to *experience*, not simply think about, God. In this goal, I wasn't so misguided as to believe I could produce a tangible sensation of the Divine. I just didn't want to miss an especially prominent spiritual opening should it occur. Part of the reason behind this was that I had remembered clearly what was said about the apostles during the Transfiguration: "Since they had stayed awake, they saw his glory" (Luke 9:32).

Then one day, as I was walking around the campus—amid this wonderful milieu and seeking to be open to a greater or new appreciation of the presence of God—I turned around and had the sense that I was face-to-face with the Divine in some vague, yet tangible, way. The interior impression passed quickly but still managed to shake me.

I knew I hadn't precipitated the encounter, because I was thinking of something else at the time. Yet I also was very grateful that the setting and my intention to embrace whatever grace came my way helped me to "be awake" so I didn't miss it. As I have found out again and again, it is easy to "step" on the graces we are given. We can do this by failing to note them, by taking them for granted, or simply by seeing them as quaint, passing, fortunate occurrences.

Bede Griffiths recognized this when he reflected on a much more dramatic spiritual encounter in his autobiography *The Golden String*:

> It is the grace given to every soul, hidden under the circumstances of our daily life, and easily lost if we choose not to attend to it. To follow up the vision which we have seen, to keep it in mind when we are thrown back again on the world, to live in its light, and to shape our lives by its law, is to wind the string into a ball and to find our way out of the labyrinth of life.

Even though my experience in this instance pales by comparison to those encountered by him and so many others—possibly including you—I felt the experience somehow had a major impact on me. The affirmation of this came as I was walking back to my townhouse and I met a Sister of Mercy who was taking courses there at the time. Upon seeing me, she immediately gave me a funny look (I think my face must have still been a bit ashen). After a brief pause, she finally asked how I was doing. When I couldn't quite reply with my usual repartee, she asked me what had happened. When I tried to explain but couldn't quite adequately do it, she invited me for coffee and we went over to the college cafeteria. It was all but empty, so we got something to drink, went over to a quiet corner, and I told my story.

As Iain Matthew, author of *The Impact of God*, rightly points out, "Any discussion of experience, particularly one's experience of God, is going to feel inadequate. Talking about an event is, after all, talk—the word 'fire' never burnt anybody." Yet, given the tender but clear interpersonal touch she had as a natural spiritual director, she helped me reexperience and seek to more fully appreciate what had happened in ways that my own defenses and fears would not quite allow. The whole experience, including the chance to reflect on it with someone whom I trusted, turned out to be an amazing grace for me.

Although we may not realize it, everyone experiences such epiphanies during life—times when life pauses, the Divine becomes evident in our everyday schedule, and we have the opportunity to become more clear as to what is truly important. In such instances, we are able to deeply feel a more powerful sense of peace or awe. In such instances, we have the opportunity to touch the holy or, more accurately, *God comes and touches us*.

This is more essential than all the theological knowledge—as important, wonderful, and instructive as it is—because such encounters can lead to a deepening of our faith and personal relationship with God. It is not surprising or radical to think that if we can be better attuned to the spaces God is making in our lives to receive the Divine, then our faith can become more real, powerful, and deeply *felt*. Moreover, because of such experiences, our compassion toward others (a major fruit of an encounter with God) will also be filled with this joy and peace. As Thomas Merton, a contemplative and Trappist monk, indicated, when we experience a sense of oneness with God, we are then impelled to respond and serve in some way appropriate for each of us (what we would refer to as "a calling"). Certainly, Mother Teresa's life is a powerful proof of this and an inspiration for us to be clearer and more detailed about the vocation God has given us. Merton indicated that most of us look for something we like to do and then ask God to bless it. However, he wondered what it would be like for us if instead of doing this we simply asked in prayer, What do you want of me, Lord?

English Benedictine Bede Griffiths was an encouraging voice in this regard as well. He wanted Christians not only to be mentally aware of their faith but also to fully experience the presence of God within their hearts. When he went to India to help inaugurate a contemplative community there, in his autobiography he admitted that he also was going on a pilgrimage to discover "the other half of my soul." The pressing question for us now is, Should we not do the same?

We do not necessarily need to physically travel to a new land to accomplish this. Instead, primarily the journey is to move more deeply within in order to make space, open up, and welcome God, as well as appreciate—especially during dark or "gray" times—how God is making a new place for the Divine within us. Essentially, we need to undertake the adventure and experience with great initiative and energy.

Using the model of John of the Cross can help in this regard. In his book *Impact of God*, Iain Matthew, an expert on the life and work of this mystic, notes,

> "What prepares the soul to be united with God is the desire for God" [quoting St. John of the Cross]. Such faith-desire is the dynamo of John's system. When the goal seems impossibly distant, he does not suggest that we settle for something more manageable. He agrees that it is distant, and says [in the following words] that desire will get us there:
>
> So the soul must desire with all her desire to come to what in this life lies beyond her mind or the capacity of her heart.
>
> It is here that the sureness of touch, which we saw John display in [his poem] *The Flame*, comes to the fore. He never backs down from his statement of divine generosity. If he anticipates readers shaking their heads ("He's gone too far this time"), there is no hint of a "Yes,

you're right, let me rephrase that." There is only a "Please believe me."

It is with this same attitude and energy that we should also see our own pilgrimage during the brief years we are on this earth. We are all called to immerse ourselves in the friendship God offers us by allowing our relations with ourselves, others, and God to be so much more than [they] may be for most of us at this point.

HEARTSTORMING: BEGINNING THE PILGRIMAGE

In 1992, I published a book, *Touching the Holy*, on the themes of ordinariness, self-esteem, and friendship. It was at this time that I initially employed the term "heartstorming." Since then, it has also appeared in print and on the Web, albeit with a different description, by others. In my original usage, I saw heartstorming as any process that enhances *spiritual* self-esteem (experiencing the presence of God within).

In this present brief book, I would like to further unpack the approach to heartstorming in an expanded, practical, and hopefully more meaningful way. The goal is to enhance the spiritual life so our approach to meeting God can become more powerfully incarnational, experiential, and relevant. Heartstorming, as a process or attitude, is designed to help us move more deeply into the present with God in all of our life, in *every* encounter.

The end result sought is to be more mindful of how the spiritual impregnates *all* of life's joys, sorrows, and even unexciting times *if* we have the eyes to see. To frame such an inner journey as this, we will first explore two themes: releasing or letting go and experiencing God in the "gray periods" of life. This is done to encourage us to both open new spiritual space in our life and help us to see that we must seek the Divine even in passing sad moments. In this way, we can begin to enable the spiritual life to really mean our entire life.

HEARTSTORMING

How we view this ongoing interior pilgrimage from this point on is as important as the journey itself. This must be emphasized from the very beginning. Thomas Merton, mentioned earlier, went out of his way to make a special point about self-understanding and openness to the changing ways grace comes to us. In his diary *A Vow of Conversation* he admits that the spiritual journey can be discouraging at times. But then he writes, "Why desperation? That is not necessary." In another place he also reminds us that "with deep faith comes deep doubt, so give up the business of suppressing doubt."

This hopeful, yet realistic, outlook is all the more relevant to those of us interested in releasing what is holding us back, opening ourselves more to new mystery, and touching the holy in deeper ways, because it encourages us to have the courage and perseverance to look at everything with the right spirit. Moreover, it helps us develop an attitude that is marked more by a sense of *intrigue*, rather than off-putting judgment, about ourselves, others, and God. This is also more encouraging than an attitude that bounces from blaming others, to negatively judging ourselves, to becoming discouraged because we believe we, or those we seek for support, have failed in some way in our responses to God's daily callings for us.

In the following pages, with the spirit of intrigue as a backdrop, I will make an effort to seek a delicate *balance between clarity and kindness* in both self-understanding and our openness to God. Clarity is important because we want to look directly at our life so we can appreciate whether we are living out of our story in the most courageous, compassionate way possible. (We all know how easy it is to somehow be caught by our own ego, personal history, culture, or attachment.) Yet, in doing so, if we seek only clarity without kindness, we may run the risk of becoming too judgmental and either inadvertently, unnecessarily hurt our own sense of self or be too negative in our view of someone else.

Likewise, if we solely seek to be kind, we will not look far enough. In addition, when we become temporarily upset, we may prematurely stop looking at the unfamiliar or unpleasant before new wisdom is able to take root. But by spiritually and psychologically holding clarity in one hand and kindness in the other, life moves from simply being a series of tasks, successes and failures, or joys and discouragements, to something so much more. With the right balance, we also will have a greater tendency to move at a pace that is neither too slow nor too ambitious but is in keeping with the graces God is bestowing that allow us to experience inner freedom in new ways.

At different times in life, most of us have glimpses of such "spiritual spaciousness." When that occurs, we feel right with the world at that moment. It may be something small like being awakened by the early summer morning sun and realizing it's Saturday—no work today. Maybe it is during a walk in the fall in a rural area surrounded by colorful leaves and the stillness of the woods, or in a big city surrounded by people bustling with great energy. Possibly it is something more dramatic like the first day of retirement after spending a lifetime of regimented service. The illustrations are endless. Be they small or momentous, the delicious freedom experienced makes us smile, lean back, relax, take a breath, and maybe seem like we are flowing with our lives for the first time because God (and life) are held lightly, yet closely. There is no grasping or avoidance of what is true and real.

In reflecting on such experiences, hopefully our ideas about letting go, opening ourselves, and experiencing God are given the chance to significantly shift from task to journey. Paul Elie touches on this reality in his well-received work *The Life You Save May Be Your Own: An American Pilgrimage*:

> A pilgrimage is a journey undertaken in the light of a story. A great event has happened; the pilgrim hears the reports and goes in search of the evidence, aspiring to be an eyewitness. The pilgrim seeks not only to confirm the experience of others firsthand but to be changed by the experience.

In this book on authors Thomas Merton, Dorothy Day, Flannery O'Connor, and Walker Percy, Elie recognized that "Emboldened by books, they set out to have for themselves the experiences they had read about." He saw in the process of pilgrimage, as they lived it out, a desire on their part to set in motion those elements that would allow secondhand knowledge to become firsthand experiences for them. Walker Percy, for example, wanted "a shift of ground, a broadening of perspective, a change of focus." In the case of Dorothy Day, she believed she "had received a call, a vocation, a direction" in her life, and, as in the case of the other three, she wanted to act on this call.

A call to inner freedom, so grace (by definition, freely given to us by God) can be embraced and experienced, is certainly akin to this. When we become deeply interested in how releasing the unnecessary and becoming open to new ways of being and experiencing can be the basis of an ongoing attitude of living, we begin trading in used gifts and experiences for the unforeseen, possibly expanded, radically different ones offered by God, but heretofore unrecognized. We are *alive*. Before this, there was limited space to welcome God and the gifts being offered. Now the story is different for us: dedication and action have replaced what was only a wistfulness as to what life might truly be like with the right actions on our part.

When questioned about the precision of his writing, that is, the difference between the right word and the almost right word, Mark Twain reportedly responded that it was tantamount to the difference between lightning and the lightning bug. Similarly, study and practice of what would encourage an attitude of inner freedom, versus merely considering, fantasizing, or romanticizing about it, represents two completely different worlds: one is partaking of the true meal of life, whether it is modest or terrific in the world's eyes, and the other is simply studying a menu of life that, even if it is very enticing, never becomes real; it is never truly nourishing to our inner life.

Yet people spend much of their life this way. One possible reason is that the search for the inner freedom produced by a dedication to the spirit of letting go and openness to the spiritual is neither easy nor magical. Instead, it requires that we be willing to ask challenging questions with as much honesty, intrigue, and clarity as possible.

Many of us have in the back of our minds a belief or desire that life could be so much more under the right circumstances. Few of us recognize though that we, ourselves, are the very ones standing in the way of this—not consciously of course, for who would do that to oneself? However, by not reflecting on the right type of questions (especially the ones that seem to strike a particularly personal chord in us), a default setting—an unspoken choice to spend a great deal of life being mired in doing just what many others are doing—can well be our fate. Yet, through prayer and reflection, there is hope, especially when we join those living in the Spirit, who are responding to the same desire for a greater awareness of the fruits of inner freedom as we are. It is all certainly worth the effort.

As Walker Percy's uncle reminded him, "There is but one good life and if [people] yearn for it and again practice it....Love and compassion, beauty and innocence will return. It is better to have breathed them an instant than to have supported inequity for a millennium. Perhaps only flames can rouse man from his apathy to his destiny."

Given this, the question for us is, What are "the flames" in our life now that may be prompting our interest in reading this book and *experiencing*, rather than merely *knowing about*, God? For the spiritual *life* to be real and full, it must be a living experience that pervades everything. When this occurs, religion is not restricted to a dead history or official prayers. Moreover, when we embrace spirituality for ourselves instead of simply mimicking what others have told us, life is not set or comfortable.

Instead, it is marked by a simplicity of purpose that involves not only new learning but constant *un*learning to make space for what is occurring *now*. It is attuned to the nuances of life that society in its search for the dramatic often misses. As Henry David Thoreau, an American essayist, naturalist, and philosopher, once cautioned, "It was easy to see destruction, which is sudden and spectacular: everyone hears the crash of a tree. But who hears the growth of a tree, the constant work of creation?"

To attend to such quiet movements in the spiritual life, we must be "spiritually mindful"—being in the present with our eyes wide open to what is happening *now* that God wants us to see afresh. One important way to accomplish this is to wake ourselves up to those elements that will prevent us from wandering purposefully through life. Two specific areas that prayerfully enable us to value the possibilities of new spiritual realities each day are *letting go* and *seeking God in the gray areas of life*. These two themes in particular can help form a new life-attitude when taken to heart. They can open us up and help us experience God in everything, even in the small disappointments we may encounter. With such an attitude in place, the other approach in this book is to experience the other half of your soul through the activity of preparing and praying over "field notes" we prepare about our own feelings, cognitions (ways of thinking, perceiving, and understanding), and experiences during the day, as well as by reflecting on those of other contemporary and classic wisdom figures we have personally encountered or who, through their writings, became our virtual mentors.

WHAT ARE SPIRITUAL "FIELD NOTES"?

Field notes, in general, are about a person's experiences of what is happening around and within them. Traditionally, they are notations made by social and behavioral scientists about what they have observed in others and themselves while undertaking research or providing treatment. For example, anthropologists have long been known for their written personal observations of cultures. Reading Margaret Mead, and, in later times, Colin Turnbull, author of *The Forest People*, enlightens us not only about the people they studied but about the researchers themselves.

Formal clinical notes or informal journal entries are similar to this. They are prepared by psychotherapists and some spiritual guides to record the course of the lives of people who come to them for assistance. They also usually offer assessments of the interventions that were recommended and the resistances to such changes encountered in the process. These findings are relevant. They speak to the helpers of their own human state and spiritual situation as well. Since all of us must face transitions, losses, and the requirement to see things in new ways as we move forward in life, this information is essential not only to others who seek some form of help but to ourselves as well.

In my own case, I recall the efforts I made to observe and fathom people's feelings, attitudes, and cognitions. I also sought to take note of their actions, spirituality, philosophies, and hesitations to act in ways that might lead to greater inner freedom, a more powerful desire to be more compassionate with others, and an openness to the ongoing revelation of God to them in new ways. I also know that in my own field and clinical notes, by putting my spiritual and psychological "fingers" on the pulse of my own feelings and thoughts during the sessions, I could not only find out a great deal about them but also about me, because of the type of reactions they elicited. (Certain people have particular effects on us, so we can begin to see patterns that can teach us a great deal about *ourselves*, as well as those with whom we interact.)

In seeking to accomplish this myself, I was fortunate enough to have Flavian Burns, Thomas Merton's final abbot, as a mentor. We met every six weeks for almost two years. I additionally sought to glean wisdom from the writings of other classic and contemporary spiritual guides in order to see how their reflections and "field notes" were driving their own self-understanding. We can especially benefit from such virtual mentors if, in our encounters, reading, and reflection, we use as spiritual lenses both a sense of the value of releasing what is holding us back and a deeper desire to touch the holy.

In doing so, greater inner freedom is there for us for the taking—*if* we really want it. All we need do is look at them more intentionally with such a purpose. In doing this, they will allow us to better incorporate helpful attitudes and activities that can have immediate and long-term impact on the amount of freedom we have in our lives. We will also position ourselves to receive and embrace whatever graces are given to us by God in the moment.

As a matter of fact, this is exactly what I kept in mind in the preparation of *Heartstorming*, since it is a book that is not meant to simply spur greater self-understanding, as important as that is. Instead, the premise and goal of this book represent much more than that. The theory whispering behind the two longer essays in part 1 and each of the following brief notes in part 2 of this book is simple: If you can't *personally experience the holy* in all aspects of your life and enhance your behavior with others, then the lesson offered will have no lasting personal meaning. The circle of grace between ourselves and God as well as ourselves and others, must be grasped for it to have an effect.

HEARTSTORMING

Therefore, the goal of each of the following spiritual notes offered is not so we will know more *about* life; each of us already have enough commentary about the way we *should* live. Instead, it is more about how we can intentionally experience and share our lives more mindfully and fruitfully now. When this occurs, the paradox of letting go becomes more clear and compelling: the more we are able to release and be aware, the more we can receive what God is offering us now. This means that no matter what happens—be it labeled "good" or "bad" (because all of us will experience both wanted and unwanted events from birth to death)—the spirit and practice of the pilgrimage toward greater inner freedom will ensure that *all* of life is met as fully and productively as possible. God will not be someone out there or only a part of our day or week, but someone very close—maybe even closer to our real selves than we are in touch with right now.

Then, when the end of life eventually comes, as it suddenly or slowly surely will, with a spirit of letting go and opening up to new experiences at the heart of our lives, we will know that the moment we are in now is being encountered as completely as possible—almost to the point of astonishing awareness at the time.

Releasing Our Grasp and Opening Up to Touch the Holy in Ever Deeper Ways:

- Is both a practice and an attitude.
- Involves small daily actions and large decisions.
- Can be fed, not distracted, by memories of past joys, as well as by possibilities for the future.
- Never ends with a final breakthrough but rather is, more accurately, a lifelong process of recognizing and embracing God's freely (and frequently!) offered grace.
- Manifests itself differently depending on one's personality and life stage.

- ◆ Is worth the time, effort, and respect we can afford understanding and incorporating it into our overall outlook and daily experience.

- ◆ Is a way of living to help us avoid wasting so much of our short, precious life by postponing fulfillment until something else happens in the future.

- ◆ Depends on a two-fold willingness to *let go* and recognize that we can learn much from the *gray times in our life.*

Greater inner freedom—and actual encounters with the Divine within—can begin now. This is so if you are willing to decide what is relevant for you (trust in your own judgment in this regard) to embrace in the two longer chapters on letting go and sadness in part 1, do the same in reflecting on the brief field notes in part 2, and possibly start preparing your own consideration of events and interactions at day's end so you can put your own spiritually inspired psychological insights and wisdom into practice in a way that makes sense for you.

The specific reward? A flexibility, openness to grace, and lightness of being that an attitude of letting go and being present in the now can bring to us for the remainder of our lives.

The cost? As a beginning, time spent in reflection on the ongoing themes in this book, the courage to change based on what is learned, and the discipline necessary not to turn back but to keep our hands on the wheel of our lives, even when it shakes.

Not a bad offer when you think about it.

Before moving on to reflect on two major themes—the big-picture field notes—in part 1, let us first intentionally honor the ever-present Spirit of God in our life. We will do this here by sitting for a few moments with the following prayer, "Come Sit by Me," to open ourselves up to appreciating how essential experiencing the Divine in our life is. We do so to respond to the question, How can I enhance an openness in my life to having God become as real as the problems and joys I face each day?

Heartstorming

Come Sit by Me

When I am tired, God says,
"Come sit by me."

I speak about the little
things that have happened to me
during the day
and I am heard.

I share my fears,
angers, doubts,
and sorrows,
and I am held.

I smile with what energy
I have left
and am gently teased.

Then when all the conversation
is over and the day has been
opened up
and emptied out,
I am ready for rest.

Nothing is solved.
Nothing is under control.
But also nothing pressing remains.

But as I go to sleep, a fleeting thought
breaks the smooth surface
of my peace:

Come Sit by Me

What would I do each night
if God didn't say,

"Come sit by me?"

From *Snow Falling on Snow* by Robert J. Wicks
(Mahwah, NJ: Paulist Press, 2001)

AUTHOR'S NOTE ON USING MATERIAL IN THIS BOOK

Part 1 is made up of two longer reflections, while part 2 comprises forty-five "field notes"—similar to blog posts these days—on leading a rich spiritual and psychological life. If you have ten or fifteen minutes to read and reflect, you may wish to read each of the essays in part 1 first. If time is tight, however, you may find it more suitable to start with part 2. If you do this, I would suggest two steps:

> **First**, please read the introduction to part 2 before any of the field notes, since it sets the stage for the briefer posts.
>
> **Then**, once this is done, don't hesitate to choose topics of interest rather than feel compelled to read through the field notes from the first through the last.

I suggest these different approaches, because I hope that you will make this book *your* book by having it touch you where you find yourself at this point in life. No matter how you approach the material, after reading, please also allow at least a minute or two to reflect on how the theme strikes you. In this way, the material written will have a greater chance to impact you in a way that you are most apt to create in your own life *a place God can call home.*

REPRODUCIBLE MATERIAL

This book includes two poems that you are free to reproduce and distribute without requesting permission, as long as you include the source: Robert J. Wicks, *Heartstorming: Creating a Place God Can Call Home* (Mahwah, NJ: Paulist Press, 2020). These are "A Place God Can Call Home" on page vi and "Find Me Again, Lord" on pages 139–40.

PART I

Two Crucial Elements in Experiencing the Other Half of Your Soul

CREATING NEW SPACE

The Amazing Paradox of Letting Go

As I look back over forty years of being a psychotherapist, spiritual companion, and supervisor of helping professionals, as well as in my reflection on the mentoring I have received, there are questions that I wish I could or would have asked. Surprisingly, they are almost all about one thing: letting go.

Maybe I didn't ask them because in pacing the session, they didn't seem appropriate. Possibly as I walked with persons on a turn in their spiritual journey, I felt the question would ask too much—and maybe that was true at the time. Or, in my own life, the questions may not have surfaced because I was afraid of where they might lead. No matter what the reason, the end result was the same: less inner freedom and a failure to fully fathom the amazing paradox of letting go in order to meet God and life in new ways.

When people speak of "releasing" or "letting go," it is often in reference to a specific desire, possession, or relationship. But while jettisoning a particular attachment can be the source of new inner "lightness," letting go is so much more than that. What this spirit offers can be an almost indescribable gift *if* it is fully understood and becomes the cornerstone of an overall attitude of freedom that is constantly renewed and experienced.

There is relief when you release your grasp, even of something that may initially have been beneficial or practical. When the timing is right, the movement toward new freedom is wonderful. But, to be honest and realistic, such a freedom is often short-lived. The room swept clean no longer remains that way. The empty space that originally opened up new opportunities for creativity, compassion, wisdom, and the experience of God in our lives soon starts to fill up again. It need not be with something bad or addictive, but it still fills, nonetheless. Our life no longer has the sense of the fresh possibility that it did for a while.

Unfortunately, the harm in this happening is not usually recognized for some time. When it is finally discovered, a sense of self-betrayal or remorse is often experienced. This feeling may even lead us to think, "I am back where I started—or even further back. What's the use!"

However, when there is a sense of openness to nurturing an attitude of releasing or letting go, even when grasping becomes temporarily prevalent again, all is not lost. There is at least an appreciation of the fact that our new free space has slowly and quietly become contaminated again. This should not be surprising because habit (or the influences from the past and the society in which one lives) can be very persuasive. Inner freedom cannot permanently be maintained. It is also why daily meditation—even for a few moments, because regularity is more important than only occasional longer periods—is not a nicety. It is necessary for a graced perspective on life, *our* life. Otherwise, the only time we will have a true perspective on life and what is essential will be when someone dies, there is illness, or loss is experienced. How foolish it is when we live like this. So much is lost or overlooked; so many graced gifts remain unopened.

Still the good news is that when we are mindful of the natural tendency to retreat to the familiar, a reservoir of integrity always remains within us that values both honesty and clarity. Paradoxically, this awareness of having pulled back again is also able to seed an even more intense desire to practice letting go anew—maybe this time with greater wisdom concerning the challenges all of us face.

When new idols and fears appear, even though we may temporarily bow to them, our spiritual pilgrimage to experiencing life and God more directly and fully never totally ceases again. The rewards of avoiding grasping and ego tight-fistedness are experienced more quickly. The loosening of one's psychological grip and being able to smile at the amount of peace and joy during the day is felt. Yes, *deeply* felt. Then everything becomes easier because the art of letting go is experienced and honored more often—not because it should be, but because to us it simply makes sense to do so.

For this to happen, knowledge, discipline, and commitment to enhance our outlook and practice with respect to opening ourselves up to life become essential companions. With this reality before us, as a way to dispel any notion of spiritual or psychological romanticism about the process being easy, automatic, or magical, we need to write our own spiritual "field notes" on letting go and touching the holy.

They are designed to put our own, as well as the experience of others (both their successes and failures), at our disposal. Our own reflections can track the ongoing unfolding of our own life since this is a simple but powerful way to learn from personal experiences and reactions.

By utilizing such information, the goal is to aid in appreciating and recording personal breakthroughs as well as the occurrence of possibly unnecessary mistakes. In the development of our own set of field notes on inner freedom, a search is immediately undertaken for what works best, given our unique backgrounds, circumstances, personality styles, and current beliefs. By unearthing this information, we can begin to more intentionally enjoy the pilgrimage to greater inner freedom to make new space for the *experience* of, and relationship with, God. We can also see that attending to flowing, rather than merely drifting, with life is such an intriguing and rewarding daily endeavor, in and of itself. Even when it is difficult and we stumble, we learn from these encounters as well. There can be an ultimate satisfaction even in failure.

SO, WHERE DO WE BEGIN?

In order to release, obviously we first need to realize that we are holding on—in terms of material possessions, our identity, and our way of interacting with others. Surprisingly, this may not be as easy as it might seem. Finding our emotional center of gravity can be elusive. For instance, what originally was truly beneficial or rewarding behavior, over time may have quietly slipped into being something quite different: *grasping*. In some cases, society may also collude with this change, making it even harder to recognize and address.

A famous Buddhist monk once recalled such an awakening in his own life. He was staring intently at a beautiful piece of pottery. Just then, his abbot walked by and said as he passed, "Stop committing adultery." The comment and observation by someone wiser and more experienced than he was concerning what was actually taking place in his heart provided new enlightenment for him. He could now see what was actually happening. It obviously had nothing to do with a sexual encounter within or outside of the monastery. It dealt instead with the fact that he had moved from admiration of a beautiful piece of pottery, which is a wonderful attitude, to a desire to *possess* the vase, something unhelpful to someone committed to inner freedom. Admiration allows us to fully enjoy and then move on. With lust we become captured by the object, person, or cause. We are caught by it in ways that prevent us from appreciating everything else that is also before us as gift.

If we went to a beautiful garden and were held by only one flower, what a waste it would be. Likewise, if we heard only one musical instrument during an overture, so much would be missed. Preferences are natural but they can easily be taken too far. The sad thing is that we often do just that with many little and large things in life and don't even know it. We become captured not only by our basic style of dealing with life but also by what seems new, different, or supposedly perfect, until it dawns on us that we have been duped by induced needs or society's salesmanship. Eventually, the new becomes familiar, the different becomes part of the same, and what was deemed perfect is finally unveiled for what or who it truly is.

So, the question we may ask is this: Why would we continue to fall for the lure of what doesn't turn out to be truly rewarding when in our hearts we actually know better? A bombardment of formal and informal advertising has replaced a psychology and philosophy of hope. Instead, an "anxiety of entitlement" and a fear that our needs won't be met unless we are aggressive on our own behalf is promulgated. Once again, though, why do we continually fall for it? After all, we are pretty bright and have had some powerful, revelatory experiences in our life, haven't we?

In his book *Ways of Seeing*, John Berger offers some guidance on this:

> Publicity speaks in the future tense and yet the achievement of this future is endlessly deferred. How then does publicity remain credible—or credible enough to exert the influence it does? It remains credible because truthfulness of publicity is judged, not by the real fulfillment of its promises, but by the relevance of its fantasies to those of the spectator-buyer. Its essential application is not to reality but to daydreams. No two dreams are the same. Some are instantaneous, others prolonged. The dream is always personal to the dreamer. Publicity does not manufacture the dream. All that it does is to propose to each one of us that we are not yet enviable—yet could be.

Rabbi Abraham Joshua Heschel, whose books reflect profound understandings of what life can offer when lived nobly, reflected on the question of "needs," as cited in *The Wisdom of Heschel,* edited by Ruth Marcus Goodhill:

> Needs are looked upon today as if they are holy....Suppression of a desire is considered a sacrilege that must inevitably avenge itself in the form of some mental disorder.... He who sets out to employ the realities of life as a means for satisfying his own desires will soon forfeit his freedom and be degraded to a mere tool. Acquiring things, he becomes enslaved to them; in subduing others, he loses his own soul. We feel jailed in the confinement of personal needs...we must be able to say no to ourselves in the name of a higher *yes.*....Every human being is a cluster of needs, some of which are indigenous to his nature, while others are induced by advertisement, fashion, envy, or come about as miscarriages of authentic needs....We usually fail

to discern between authentic and artificial needs and, mis-judging a whim for an aspiration, we are thrown into ugly tensions. Most obsessions are the perpetuation of such misjudgments. In fact, more people die in the epidemics of needs than in the epidemics of disease.

In these words, he is following up on his famous dictum: "What I look for is not how to gain a firm hold on myself and on life, but primarily how to live a life that would deserve and evoke an eternal Amen."

Heschel obviously appreciates the fact that we must begin to see (1) how we have confined our identity to our perceived needs and (2) where the centers of gravity in our days are. In the process of responding to this call to see these truths, we must ask ourselves:

- Where have I imprisoned my identity within my needs?
- Are these needs really the most important things in my life?
- Are these the areas worthy of my life and ones to which I want to give most of my attention?

The true search for inner freedom is *not* for the romantic or those who fanaticize. It is for those who truly want what is left of their lives to be a real journey in living. In addition, by reflecting on the aspects of the process, the fuse can be lit to see both how exciting and meaningful letting go can be.

Cultivating a Spirit of Letting Go By...

- ◆ Attending to the spirit and process of letting go each day.
- ◆ Undertaking a willingness to take risks, be coura-geous, and unlearn what may have been valid but is now stale.
- ◆ Recognizing the enchantment and vitality of experi-menting with life and the way we approach people, premises, and desires.

- ◆ Incorporating a childlike playful nature and right brain sense of the world and yourself, rather than being captured by an image of adulthood that is deadening.

- ◆ Encouraging a desire to expand your repertoire as a way of exploring a broader self-narrative rather than confining the voice to what others or society has thus far dictated it to be.

- ◆ Having the discipline to pursue a spirit of "releasing" in all aspects of life.

- ◆ Being a learner all through life by taking practical steps to be open, observe clearly and nonjudgmentally, and absorb the cardinal virtue of psychological sages through the centuries: *humility*.

- ◆ Seeking friends who encourage and also practice a commitment to inner freedom.

- ◆ Choosing and emulating a person who models a life based on "letting go" to act as a human compass.

- ◆ Retrieving memories of when you felt truly free, as though you were flowing with life rather than merely meeting certain dictates.

CHANGING THE MEMORY YOU HAVE OF YOURSELF

Releasing also involves more than letting go of things or attachments to others. It has to do with Jesus's call to put on the new person. To accomplish this, we must be willing to change the limited memory we have of ourselves. In his book *A Path with Heart*, psychologist and spiritual teacher Jack Kornfield shares the following story:

An older man, a lifetime smoker, was hospitalized with emphysema after a series of small strokes. Sitting beside his bed, his daughter urged him, as she had often done, to give up smoking. He refused and asked her to buy him more cigarettes. He told her, "I'm a smoker this life, and that's how it is." But several days later he had another small stroke, apparently in one of the memory areas of the brain. Then he stopped smoking for good—but not because he decided to. He simply woke up one morning and forgot that he was a smoker.

To this, Kornfield adds with a sense of simple directness, "We do not have to wait for a stroke to learn to let go." However, when we see that our true identity is being compromised by something, maybe what we do need is a "spiritual stroke" that awakens us to the fact that we need not be chained to an identity.

The same can be said of our identity when it is tied to the reputation we have with others. When I read a dialogue between a master and disciple in the book *One Minute Wisdom* by Anthony deMello, a recognition dawned of how foolish all of us are to be tied to this reputation. In the story, the master's disciples knew that he was quite impervious to what people thought of him, so they asked him how he had gained such inner freedom. In response, he laughed aloud and said,

Till I was twenty I did not care what people thought of me. After twenty I worried endlessly about what my neighbors thought. Then one day after fifty I suddenly saw that they hardly ever thought of me at all!

There must be a decision to let go of one's concern—whether it is reasonable or not—as to what people think about the changes that such inner freedom can produce. In a broader sense, we can see that the issue of who is the holder of the rights to our own story is an important issue to be resolved when addressing letting go and inner freedom. Terry Hershey in his enchanting book *The Power of Pause* tells the following story about a girl labeled as "difficult" that makes this point clearly:

> In the 1930s when Gillian was a child, her teachers considered her learning disabled, one of those students who didn't pay attention or focus, and who could not sit still. ADHD was not yet a diagnosis, so Gillian was labeled "difficult." And her parents were deeply troubled.
>
> A school counselor arranged a meeting with Gillian and her parents to discuss the options. Through the entire meeting, Gillian sat on her hands, stoic, doing her best to act natural and well-behaved. At the end, the counselor asked to see Gillian's parents privately, outside the office. Before he left the room, he turned on his radio. Music filled the office. Outside the office door, the counselor asked Gillian's parents to look back inside at their daughter. No longer seated, Gillian now moved about the room with the music—free, untroubled, and blissful.
>
> "You see," the counselor told the parents, "your daughter isn't sick. She's a dancer."
>
> This story could have gone another way. Gillian could have been labeled and medicated. Problem solved.
>
> Instead, she was given the freedom to live from the inside out. The result? A lifetime of dance on stage and in films, and an extensive career as choreographer for such shows as *Cats* and *The Phantom of the Opera*. Difficult little Gillian became the great Gillian Lynne.

Spirituality has long addressed the importance of *imago Dei*, that is, recognizing that we are all made in the image and likeness of God, and psychology supports this through the approach called "narrative therapy." It is worth taking a few moments to understand some key tenets of this approach as one way to respond to the call by God for us to *make all things new*—especially ourselves.

BEING OPEN TO CHANGING OUR NARRATIVE

In Parker Palmer's book *Let Your Life Speak*, he reflects on the favorable elements of his own life when he notes that "the life I am living is not the same as the life that wants to live in me....I had started to understand that it is indeed possible to live a life other than one's own....I had simply found a 'noble' way to live that was not my own, a life spent imitating heroes instead of listening to my heart."

On a more dramatic note, actress Liv Ullman once shared the following related, deeply felt sentiment regarding her own narrative:

> I am learning that if I just go on accepting the framework for life that others have given me, if I fail to make my own choices, the reasons for my life will be missing. I will be unable to recognize that which I have the power to change. I refuse to spend my life regretting the things I failed to do.

What Palmer and Ullman are both struggling with is the narrative of their lives. A creative approach to achieving a healthier, richer sense of self is with *narrative therapy*. Learning a few things from this psychological school of thought can certainly aid in supporting our spiritual journey to be open to Jesus's desire to "make all things new" in our lives.

Narrative therapy as a process is associated with the groundbreaking work of Michael White and David Epston. They were interested in how people's life stories attributed to them, but not by them, were problematic. In one of their key maxims, "the person is not the problem, the problem is the problem." The problem is a function of a labeling that overshadows alternative stories of possibility that people have within themselves but may not be in touch with at the time.

This is not simply the case in clinical settings but in how we perceive life, *our* lives, in all settings. Once again, in the words of educator and author Parker Palmer,

When we lose track of true self, how can we pick up the trail? One way is to seek clues in stories from our younger years, years when we lived closer to our birthright gifts. A few years ago, I found some clues to myself in a time machine of sorts. A friend sent me a tattered copy of my high school newspaper....[I said in it] that I would become a naval aviator and then take up a career in advertising.

I was indeed "wearing other people's faces," and I can tell you exactly whose they were. My father worked with a man who had once been a navy pilot. He was Irish, charismatic, romantic, full of the wild blue yonder and a fair share of the blarney and I wanted to be like him. The father of one of my boyhood friends was in advertising, and though I did not yearn to take on his persona, which was too buttoned-down for my taste, I did yearn for the fast car and other large toys that seemed to be the accessories of his selfhood!

These self-prophecies now over forty years old, seem wildly misguided for a person who eventually became a Quaker, a would-be pacifist, a writer, and an activist. Taken literally, they illustrate how early in life we can lose track of who we are. But inspected through the lens of paradox, my desire to become an aviator and an advertiser contain clues to the core of true self that would take many years to emerge: clues, by definition, are coded and must be deciphered....From the beginning, our lives lay down clues to selfhood and vocation, though the clues may be hard to decode. But trying to interpret them is profoundly worthwhile—especially when we are in our twenties or thirties or forties, feeling profoundly lost, having wandered, or been dragged, far away from our birthright gifts.

Narrative Therapy Skills

Narrative therapy encourages the very skills that all of us need to have in opening up our perspective as to who we are, can be, and how we might live each day. This includes our vocation and long-term goals. Some skills worth practicing with these goals in mind include the following:

- Listening to our hopes, dreams, and ideas so they are not eclipsed or crushed by the attitudes of culture, family, work, or our own previously limited self-definition

- Reflecting on those "little" events and experiences that gave and give us joy so they can be given further opportunities for expression

- Having a chance to reframe our difficulties in light of possibly unexplored gifts and talents

- Giving ourselves the power to author our own stories, since we in seeking God's sense of us—not others—hold the "copyright" to our identity

- Being sensitive to our self-talk (what we mentally tell ourselves about events, people, and ourselves) in order to pick up interpretations and criticism that are not centered in us but in the outside world's set of values and ethics

- Opening ourselves to an array of stories that color our lives but have been underrated (volunteer work may not be considered "important" because the culture doesn't seem to value unpaid activities, but after exploration *we* may see the good that we are doing and the joy it may be bringing us)

- Participating in spiritual and psychological rituals and activities that reinforce and stabilize new, more life-giving identities that reflect God's call

Narrative therapeutic views help us to see more and more of life anew in ways that help our perspective to become more open to possibility. This is done by isolating assumptions we have about ourselves, examining them, and considering alternative views, especially ones developed by *us* and not merely a mimicking of other authority figures (e.g., parents, educators, the predominant culture, therapists) no matter how noble their intentions may be.

Stephen Madigan, author of a small work called *Narrative Therapy*, notes,

> From the beginning, a central poststructural tenet of narrative therapy was the idea that we as persons are "multistoried."...Simply stated, narrative therapists took up the position that within the context of therapy, there could be numerous interpretations about persons and problems....And the very interpretations of persons and problems that therapists bring forward are mediated through prevailing ideas held by our culture regarding the specifics of who and what these persons and problems are and what they represent (abnormal/normal, good/ bad, worthy/unworthy).

Madigan recognized that people have a reputation with themselves that is very much in line with prevailing ideologies, and, in the extreme, prejudices or opinions that have nothing to do with their own values. The goal of narrative therapy is to look at many stories and interpretations in people's lives so they can resist being cast in a way that has possibly held them back. This is exactly what we should wish for ourselves and put into practice by embracing a healthy perspective on life and an openness to new views and necessary change.

Furthermore, the surprises that exploring our own narrative can provide not only open us up to expanding our own self-views and horizons, but also set the stage for undertaking a fuller appreciation of the essential role of *openness*. We thereby expand our own narrative and redefine our story—not according to the world, not according to our culture or family, and maybe not even according to our own existing view of ourselves. Part of letting go includes releasing the image we now have of ourselves as Abram and Sarai did so we can experience the other half of our soul. The following are but a few ways to do this:

Re-authoring our conversations involves identifying and attending to those parts of our life that are not in the forefront, may be neglected, or have been discouraged by others, and maybe eventually by you. **Practice:** Bring into the forefront stories of faithfulness to what is good, joys, interesting activities, positive spiritual encounters, and actions worth being happy about that are now in the shadows of your awareness.

Bring into greater awareness new balanced story lines other than the ones you or others usually tell about you. **Practice:** Use a psychological approach similar to the dermatological one of if it is wet, dry it; if it is dry, wet it. In other words, if people see you as an introvert, reflect on those times and places where you have been outgoing; if you are characterized or think of yourself as an extrovert, reflect and highlight those times during the day, week, and life where you are more contemplative, quiet, and reflective in nature.

Develop a list of favorable conditions for the under-enjoyed parts of yourself to develop further. **Practice:** Assemble a prospectus of those actions. Start with the small steps first, which, if enacted, would enrich your life and enhance your story line. For each action, also list what factors would encourage success in taking these steps.

Reflect on persons in your life who saw you differently or in a more positive light and therefore interacted with you in ways that brought out other interpersonal elements that are present but often are under-expressed. **Practice:** Recall specific people who did this and image them in your life now. Then imagine being invited to practice in other settings so your identity can be more directly shaped by their increased expression by you.

Risk seeing yourself in different ways other than how you and others view you now or had viewed you before. **Practice:** Picture yourself describing the adventure of seeing yourself and practicing different behaviors not normally attributed to you. For example, if you are seen by others as a workaholic, practice taking time during the day to enjoy a leisurely walk and image having encouraging people from your past rejoicing with you in your living a more balanced life.

Seek to appreciate more and more that recognizing and responding to negative messages you have received about yourself (maybe even from yourself) is an essential part of balancing your own story and making the perspective you have on your life more accurate. **Practice:** Write down attempts made by people—even those who seemingly meant well—to instill fear, shame, guilt, hopelessness, discouragement of initiative, helplessness, or unreasonable and unhelpful perfectionism (as opposed to being inspired to reach higher goals). After this, write down stories of experiences of courage, stamina, self-improvement, self-understanding, forgiveness, initiative, and recall those in your life who reinforced positive narratives. (Include passages of Sacred Scripture and spiritual writings that have done this as well for you.)

Michael White's *Re-Authoring Lives: Interviews and Essays* and *Narrative Therapy in Practice* (edited by Monk, Winslade, Crocket, and Epston), *Narrative Therapy* by Freedman and Combs, and Madigan's *Narrative Therapy* all offer broader and more in-depth treatment of practices in expanding your narratives.

When we seek to take the psychological approach of narrative therapy, we are using psychology to set the spiritual stage for *metanoia*. By this I mean a true "conversion"—in other words, a continual repentance that is not marked by tears so much as by a willingness to release or let go so we can embrace an identity more in line with how God, rather than the world, sees us. To seek such a sense of self as this is a true cornerstone of experiencing "the other half of your soul" and, in the process, meeting God and life in radically new and renewing ways. No matter what is going on in life at the time—even when encountering the gray times which we would normally want to avoid or forget—we will realize that an opportunity is before us to go deeper and spiritually experience more of life.

MY SOUL IS TIRED

Gaining New Spiritual Wisdom during Life's "Gray Times"

> Don't turn away. Keep your gaze on the bandaged place. That's where the light enters.
>
> —Rumi

> And once the storm is over, you won't remember how you made it through, how you managed to survive. You won't even be sure whether the storm is really over. But one thing is certain. When you come out of the storm, you won't be the same person who walked in. That is what this storm's all about.
>
> —Haruki Murakami

> There are as many nights as days, and the one is just as long as the other in the year's course. Even a happy life cannot be without a measure of darkness, and the word "happy" would lose its meaning if it were not balanced by sadness.
>
> —Carl Jung

The dark night of the soul and psychological depression have received a great deal of attention over the years. Within these dramatic movements in life, the experience of a palpable void in life naturally attracts a great deal of interest, as well it should. However, the Spirit of God appears in the "gray" times in our lives as well. Yet attention to these fleeting moments, hours, or longer periods hasn't attracted as much attention. This is a shame, since much can be gained if we don't merely ignore, play down, or wait until the "low" times in life pass. As a part of experiencing God in all of life, we must perceive the numerous ways sadness can become more deeply "spiritual" (meaningful in new ways) in our life.

Such a positive movement is possible when we *intentionally* bring God into those times in our day and life that are difficult, disappointing, troubling, confusing...or sad. Given this, exploration of those—sometimes almost fleeting—periods when we don't quite feel ourselves should be part of our daily journey. Within our unwanted feelings may be a calling worth listening to, not only to alleviate the negative experiences but also to open new possibilities of learning from them. Surprisingly, such possibilities for personal deepening may even be ones that *would not have been possible had the occasions of sadness not occurred in the first place.* While it is foolish to desire sadness or the events that cause them, when they do make their appearance, as they surely will, it would seem just as foolish to not take the steps to benefit from them in some way. In the words of Anne Morrow Lindberg,

> I do not believe that sheer suffering teaches. If suffering alone taught, all the world would be wise, since everyone suffers. To suffering must be added mourning, understanding, patience, love, openness and the willingness to remain vulnerable.

Sadness, disappointments, rejections, and other gray times in our day and life need to be brought to prayer and quiet reflection. In doing this, the themes can be taken to heart, pondered on a walk, or shared in a discussion with an old friend. On another level, they will also prompt us when guiding others to encourage them to be more sensitive to the question of where sadness might be leading them in their lives as well.

Another benefit of facing and reflecting on sadness and suffering is that it can also help us to avoid falling into the pitfalls of simply blaming others for all of our negative feelings and leaving it at that. Further, it will allow us to seek to *nonjudgmentally*, clearly but gently, understand our own possible role in what led to sadness.

For us to learn about ourselves in this way, it must be done without indicting ourselves in the process. Berating ourselves about a failure does nothing positive. It can even lead to further unnecessary self-inflicted wounds because the reality is that the behavior that you wince at will eventually turn into behavior that you wink at because you can't constantly pick on yourself. As a matter of fact, turning on ourselves may only lead to a level of frustration that causes us to drop our self-exploration: "This is how I am; I can do nothing about it." Whereas, looking at our sense of sadness in the right way can lessen such discouragement and shorten periods of feeling lost or hurt. A sense of intrigue about where God is leading me *within* the experience, however, can transform the process and goal into a helpful interior journey.

The pain we experience at the hands of others (or ourselves for that matter) is also often unintentionally lengthened when we don't think about what has happened in a helpful way. A healthy spiritual perspective involves being as clear as possible about our thoughts, feelings, beliefs, and actions. Yet simultaneous with clarity and facing unpleasant feelings and thoughts directly, we recognize such an honest inner exploration needs to be done with a deep sense of God's abiding love. Accordingly, sometimes, in our seeking to explore our sadness we may unearth a new recognition of how little we *truly* believe in God's love deep in our hearts—no matter what we have been saying to ourselves and others to the contrary. Such a lack of belief in God's love certainly is something that needs to be brought to prayer and to the discussions we have with those to whom we turn for guidance or who are sources of informal wisdom. This isn't possible though if we don't know that we feel this way.

Despite the advantages just noted, there is an important caution in facing our gray times that must be recognized if our efforts are to be real and true. It is this: in seeking the spiritual gifts that sadness can bring, if we seek to circumvent or shorten the pain felt, we will simply be fooling ourselves and using religious language to do it.

The grace of new wisdom that comes from seeking God is not beyond, but *amid*, the sadness. It is not possible to deeply learn and change within if we simply seek to "spiritualize" what we are feeling or has happened. Yet this is what we risk doing when we simply put religious words to a troubling experience without facing the source of the sorrow directly and completely.

I once read back-to-back reflections by two women religious who had experienced sexual abuse as children. One, filled with compassion and hope, evidenced she had faced and walked with God—and at times felt that God wasn't with her—through depression and anger, and the sense of loss that abuse usually causes. The other was a flowery, pietistic reflection that seemed to indicate she was using religious imagery to get around the pain, rather than encountering her feelings and thoughts with God at her side. Avoidance and denial are not the vehicles of a spiritual approach to mine our sadness. Honesty, openness, and hope are.

Another important reality about the transformation of sadness into spiritual wisdom is that not only can we deepen in the process, but it may also allow us to enable others to feel the healing presence of God in ways we couldn't have before. I have an example of that quite close to home to illustrate this.

My daughter was diagnosed with severe scoliosis when she was very young. This meant wearing a removable cast twenty-three hours each day for almost three years. When that didn't work, she needed to have thirteen levels of her spine fused and a steel rod inserted to keep the spine straight until the bones fused. Following this in college, after experiencing pain that would immobilize her, she had to then have the rod surgically removed. The problem did not end there, as chronic pain and health scares follow her to this day.

Amid all these ups and downs, she surprised me one day with the statement, "I didn't tell you this before, but I always wanted to be a U.S. Marine Corps officer like you were, Dad. However, because of my physical condition, I knew it would never be possible."

"So, what have you decided to do, given this desire and the fact that you can't follow through as you had dreamed you would?" I asked.

She responded, "I have decided to become a social worker and work in the Veterans Administration with military personnel when they return from war." She did follow through on this commitment and now works with severely injured returning veterans from both the Iraqi and Afghani conflicts. They are often persons who are psychologically traumatized or missing a leg or arm. Because she has taken her own injuries and suffering to prayer, she is ready to welcome them in ways others who have not experienced spiritual sadness could not—including me, whose life's work includes aiding helpers, healers, and members of the military deal with their trauma.

For example, recently when approached by a veteran new to her caseload, she warmly welcomed him as she does all who come in for help. He responded by saying, "Boy, you are in high spirits." To this she responded softly, "You have served our country well. Now come on in and let us know what we can do for *you*."

She and others like her prove that sadness need not be the last word for us. Instead it may actually be the *first* word in embracing new insights and healing that will impact not only us but those who come to us for solace and support.

We need to realize that taken individually most aspects of the gray times in our lives are not new or dramatic. By themselves they provide no great teaching. Yet it is my belief that taken together, with the intention of seeing more clearly where God is seeking to meet us during the gray times of life, they may spur helpful new spiritual wisdom—wisdom that in the past we may have either missed or forsaken in our rush to move away from the negative events, feelings, and thoughts that occur at points in all our lives. Exploration of such negative experiences helps us to bring God more into the center of the important aspects of our lives. They are crucial to experiencing the other half of our soul and sensing God walking with us in tangible ways.

STRUCK BY SADNESS

Annie Dillard in *An American Childhood* wrote, "My feelings deepened and lingered. The swift moods of early childhood—each formed by and suited to its occasion—vanished. Now feelings lasted so long they left stains. They arose from nowhere, like winds or waves, and battered me or engulfed me." There are times when seemingly out of the blue I feel a bit down. Sometimes I don't know the cause. Other times it simply may arise because a random thought strikes me that I have not been a better person. Strange, in such cases, how the experience seems to come out of nowhere rather than being tied to a specific failing or mistake. When this happens, I might think to myself, "I should have been more gentle, less greedy or narcissistic, more accepting of others."

Such thoughts are both a temptation and an invitation. The *temptation* is to simply become discouraged and filled with a sense of shame, rather than guilt over a particular failing. In the case of shame, it is not that I have done something wrong. Rather, in the case of shame, it is *I* am *someone* wrong. Shame can produce such an overwhelming sense of inadequacy and failure that it is both spiritually and psychologically dangerous if left unaddressed.

Still, the paradoxical grace is that the *invitation* stands alongside the temptation. Moreover, it is *because* we have had such a negative experience that we are now offered a chance to meet God in new ways, if we tend to it gently and clearly.

In the case of guilt or shame, the sadness we experience at the very least is asking us to recall John 15:15 in a deeper more personal way. This passage is where Jesus addresses his disciples then, and us now, to embrace his words more deeply: *You are my friend.*

The friendship offered by Jesus helps us realize that sadness about feeling a sense of failure as a person can actually result in our turning to him with greater energy and interest. Maybe it will result in our adopting a gospel, so we can slowly learn a lesson or two from each chapter by heart. In this way, we can mentally walk through that gospel before we get out of bed in the morning, possibly on a walk during the day, or before we fall asleep.

In addition, when we walk more closely with Jesus, we still will feel guilt or shame, but with prayerful reflection on John 15:15, rather than pulling us into the past and leaving us there, we are alerted to the need for grace in the present so we can greet the future more compassionately.

In such a case, in going forward, sadness will not simply be a gray period to ignore, feel badly during, or fight, but a quiet time to *remember*. Remember what? Remember the unconditional love of God and to relish in it while learning to make possible changes on how we lead our life now. This may wind up as having impact on us for the good for longer than the sad moment. It may also encourage us to set aside at least a few moments each day, after reading a few lines from Sacred Scripture, to sit peacefully in the downtimes of our life so we can regain a healthy perspective on even the toughest issues. Knowing of God's deep love and trusting in it can do that for us even when we feel there is no answer to what we feel.

If we approach the feeling carefully, sadness that seems to appear out of nowhere can give us the impetus to move our relationship with God out of the general arena. Instead, it can impel us to embrace God in the Gospels and other New Testament readings more intently as a way of seeking a divine encounter that is more compelling. Real spirituality dawns when God becomes as real as the problems that we face each day. Certainly, sadness is one of those "problems" to include and examine carefully with an eye to the place God has in our daily life. Such instances include those times when we receive harsh criticism or encounter inadvertent suffering.

IMPURE CRITICISM

All criticism is impure. Even if it is 99 percent for good reasons, there is still that small piece of it that was not for mature or helpful reasons. When we offer it to others, we feel we may be helping them become aware of an injustice done to us. Even so, it is like old forms of chemotherapy in that it destroys the "good cells," as well as "the bad." We not only provide helpful information, but also hurt the good spirit that may be connected with it.

In my own case, one of the gifts I feel God has given me to share is my passion and enthusiasm. However, sometimes when I am this way, I say or do things without considering the timing or person I am sharing it with. As a result, I hurt them, and if they share with me what I have done, it makes me sad in the moment as well.

Because criticism is never pure, there is a temptation at that time to condemn the messenger and say that the person is hurting me because of their own failings. While this is sometimes true to some extent, the danger is to simply blame the critic. Such projection of blame is very immature and helps no one. Another temptation is to be too hard on myself. Rather than being helpful, such self-condemnation is no more helpful than projecting blame on the other. Discouragement is yet a third temptation, since failings are often tied to the very gifts we have, so it is easy to make the same mistake over and over.

To the contrary, what prayer and a sense of feeling loved by God do in that situation can really be magnificent. When criticism is received, it can provide several opportunities, including these:

Learning to be gracious in apologizing for the mistake and the hurt felt by another;

Knowing not to take responsibility for the full amount of upset experienced, because that is the result of a number of factors within the person offering the criticism; and

Getting a chance to see more clearly where you need to "prune" your gifts so that they are delivered in the right measure, at the right time, and with a clearer understanding of the relationship. In my spontaneity, for example, I often get so exuberant that I share ideas with others without laying the relational groundwork or being sensitive enough to the interpersonal setting, and in the process inflict harm. Whereas, if I had done it when the relationship was firmer or the timing more private, it might possibly have been helpful. Yet the bottom line remains: If I drop a rock on your head on purpose or by mistake, you still get a bump. No excuses. Just learning to do better and moving on is called for.

Given the above learning that is possible with the right attitude, another advantage is a better recognition of when and how to offer my criticism of others. Knowing how criticism hurts me, it gives me pause whether I should make it at all, and if so, how I should frame it. I also need to take a clear look at my own many motivations, that is, seeking to find the impure ones that are certainly there as well as my "noble" ones, before offering or formulating my comments.

When I am faithful to this, I find that I tend to give less haphazard feedback, and when I do, it is by framing it with a sense of understanding rather than indignant blame. In doing this, I must confess, I don't feel any less sad. I do feel that God is softening my soul, however, so that I am more understanding of other people's reasons to criticize, and I'm more careful in offering my own. Will I fail others and myself again? Surely. Maybe I will catch myself a bit more quickly, however, and be a bit more forgiving of those who don't wish to see that critical feedback is not as cut and dry as it might seem.

INADVERTENT SUFFERING

Sometimes people we know fail to realize the suffering they have caused in us or we fail to recognize the suffering we have caused in them. Yet such suffering when it is prayed with and reflected on need not be the final word. The following demonstrates this in a reflection shared by a priest friend of mine on Mother's Day. It shows how sadness can truly blossom into wisdom when we embrace, rather than run away from, those instances where we have inadvertently caused suffering in another person.

A Reflection

Mother's Day is special, but I learned years ago to be cautious about it. I was a new priest—my 1st assignment—and I gave what I thought was a stem-winder of a Mother's Day homily. This woman, who later became a dear friend, pulled me aside to tell me that she wanted children but couldn't have them and how difficult Mother's Day was for her. I later learned that her mother abused her terribly—physically and emotionally. So, since then, I get that today is complicated.

This morning I corresponded with a dear friend who wanted to be a mother but couldn't. She is one of the most generative people I know. She has given life to so many, often to those who thought they had nothing and no one and nowhere to go. I know this isn't all that it means to be a mother, or a substitute for it, but she has embraced the grace to make her loss into a gain for others. That's a mother!

Pray that my friend keeps being her gracious, generative self. We need many more like her in the world. Think of all the great religious sisters whom we know and love and have been mothered by—wow!

How fortunate it was that the woman in the pews was able to share her pain. It was done to unburden herself and share the nuances of what seems simple and good on the surface. Just as fortunate though was the nondefensiveness and openness of the priest to see anew the different aspects of even celebrations of something wonderful like motherhood. Once again, with prayer, reflection, and openness to learn, the presence of God can be made known through the words of others and our own embracing of the movements of other people's lives as well as our own.

This is not a guarantee if we don't realize our role in other people's pain. In another instance, a young preacher was extolling the callings of marriage and becoming a priest or vowed religious. After his reflection at Mass, a middle-aged man tearfully approached him and said, "But you never mentioned the committed single life?" To this, the preacher said, "It is not a calling recognized in the Catholic Church."

He had no sense of what the Church has spoken about this calling but more than that, he had no sense of the man's pain. Very sad for the man who approached him. Sad even for the young person in ministry, not to see the opportunity that presented itself as did the priest above when the woman approached him on Mother's

Day after his homily. If the movement toward enabling sadness to become spiritual has an arch enemy, it is personal defensiveness and arrogance—especially, when the person is not able to see its harm.

Some other specific triggers of sadness, discouragement, and suffering that come our way, even though they may not seem significant at the time but are worth exploring if we wish to really give sadness the opportunity to be transformed into spiritual wisdom, include such experiences as the following:

Cultural alienation: A woman religious once said to me, "I am an Italian American in an Irish American religious congregation. I just don't fit."

Inadvertent rebuffs: As Brother David Steindl-Rast illustrates in his book *Gratefulness, the Heart of Prayer*: "You notice someone smiling at you; gratefully you acknowledge the smile by smiling back. Then something does not seem quite right. You turn around and notice that behind you stands someone for whom that smile was actually meant. It hurts, doesn't it? No big trauma, of course. But we can imagine that someone whose feelings were hurt repeatedly, especially during childhood, may be permanently injured."

The demands of transitions: In her novel *The Little Paris Bookshop*, Nina George writes insightfully about change in the following scene: "My little big friend Samy left me with one final scrap of wisdom. For once she didn't shout—she tends to shout. She gave me a hug as I sat there, staring at the sea and counting the colors, and whispered very quietly to me: 'Do you know that there's a halfway world between each ending and each new beginning? It's called the hurting time, Jean Perdu. It's a bog; it's where your dreams and worries and forgotten plans gather. Your steps are heavier during that time. Don't underestimate the transition, Jeanno, between farewell and new departure. Give yourself the time you need. Some thresholds are too wide to be taken in one stride.'"

Discouragement: Mary Anne Radmacher aptly calls us to move ahead when we feel a bit down and discouraged by noting, "Courage doesn't always roar. Sometimes courage is the little voice at the end of the day that says I'll try again tomorrow."

Anxiety about facing aspects of life: By remembering the kind words of others we can use them to spiritually prop open the doors more widely to the inner places we may be called to visit more often but may leave closed, maybe even tightly shut at times. Places and experiences of gratitude, gentleness, attentiveness to what is truly important may not be valued by the world but can be our true "Advent places" that will prepare us to spiritually receive what we do not yet have, know, or recognize as being of meaning and value for us.

Ego-centered wounds: These wounds are caused because we are driven by our desire to build ourselves up rather than respond to the call to build up something greater than ourselves.

There are also many other triggers to experiences of sadness. Lack of gratitude by others, rejection, misunderstandings, a failure to meet expectations (our own and others), jealousy, self-blame, loneliness, loss, missed opportunities, a lack of respect, competition, hidden pride, broken trust, ridicule, not being taken seriously, cowardice, illness, and the absence of appreciation by others of our gifts and joys. The list is endless, as is the opportunity to not simply take them to heart but also to take them to prayer so they may lead somewhere that will soften our soul. This will help both deepen and make us more compassionate. Moreover, it may also uncover a new side to our relationship with God.

At the very least, when we seek to see sadness as a more integral part of our daily pilgrimage to find God more intimately, rather than simply viewing downtimes as a "one off" experience to escape, avoid, or ignore, we can open ourselves to appreciate the following tenet of the spiritual life in a possibly deeper way than ever before:

No matter *what* happens,
no matter *when* it happens,
we are not alone.

Instead, in the gray times, God is with us in continually
    new ways
if only we have the eyes to see.

Enabling our sadness to become spiritual
means seeking to open those eyes to love anew.

The grace is there for this to become so,
but it is up to us to reach out to fully embrace it.

Given this, the question for us remains: *Will we?*

If we do, these times can be termed "spiritual sadness" because they are not simply unwanted psychological cul de sacs. Instead, they are experiences that can be termed "spiritual" now because they are being included in ways close to our heart where we can experience God's call to us. They are other ways to *experience* the other half of our soul in the now. The gray times in life can sometimes offer that in ways unopen to us in other types of experiences.

PART II

"You Got This!"

Introduction
PARTNERING
WITH GOD

A Word of Encouragement

Fear, doubt, loneliness, and the need for a sense of courage that is based on a simple faith and good friendship are what all of us must encounter at times in the spiritual life. Nobel laureate and holocaust survivor Elie Wiesel once quipped, "When you see an angel of the Lord coming with the words, 'Be not afraid,' you know you are in trouble!" An honest, fully lived, and embraced spiritual life includes major challenges.

It also includes times of serious questioning. This is to be expected and faced. Once again, as Thomas Merton aptly recognized, "With deep faith comes deep doubt, so give up the business of suppressing doubt."

Finally, in participating in a rich spiritual life, there will be a sense of aloneness at times as well. A priest who knew this, led a liturgy for children on the Feast of the Immaculate Conception. He told the young people present that the appearance of an angel of the Lord to Mary, the Mother of Jesus, in the Annunciation was a very dramatic encounter for her. However, after the angel left and Mary was all by herself, there was also the probable emotional hurdle of feeling alone while facing what she was being called to do and be. He then asked the children present what they would say to Mary to help her through this possible sense of isolation.

In response, one young girl immediately raised her hand. When the priest saw this and asked her what she would say to Mary to make her feel better, the young girl told him she would say to her at that tender moment: "You got this!"

When you are going through a difficult time in life, with simple faith, good friendship, and courage, please remember: "You got this!"

Just after 4:00 a.m. one morning, I awoke from a dream of abandonment with an aching emotion of loneliness. The dream involved my sitting in the back of a long, black limousine waiting to be driven somewhere. On an impulse, I decided to get out for a bit to stretch my legs. There was snow on the ground and I trod carefully so I didn't get my shoes too wet. After walking for only a few moments, it occurred to me that I didn't want the limousine to leave without me. I crossed the street and returned to where it was parked.

As I approached, I saw it was pulling away. I waved to the driver. He smiled and, as he drove by me, somehow I sensed in the dream that he was telling me that he was going to pull over where the sidewalk was straight. Then I could more easily step in. Instead, however, he kept on going. When I realized this, I waved to him so he could see me in the rearview mirror, but he kept going until he was out of sight.

At this point I woke up feeling an aching sense of loneliness. My mind told me that this was silly since I had both family and friends who loved me. Yet the feeling remained like a low mournful tune that only I could hear. With this music playing in my heart, I then began to look for lyrics to match: How were people letting me down and I failing them? Would there always be a certain distance between me and those whom I cherished that would be a permanent divide that could and would never be traversed? Such questions often then lead to even broader ones, and it did for me as I looked forward and remembered an Eastern philosopher writing that the last journey is taken in single file. A tone of quiet despair now seemed to pervade the dark room as I lay there.

Emotions felt just before dawn while you are half asleep can be especially valuable *if* you let them. Unlike during the day when we are on guard, in a dreamlike state, what is referred to in the field of psychology as a state of diminished consciousness, there is little, if any, ability to run away or play down what is experienced. If we greet what we feel with sensitivity and openness, we can learn much spiritually that can enable us to become closer to God, who is always available to us.

In the case of this dream, I felt urged on to sit with what I was feeling by recalling the following words from Rainer Maria Rilke's *Letters to a Young Poet*:

> All emotions are pure which gather you and lift you up; that emotion is impure which seizes only *one* side of your being and so distorts you....And your doubt may become a good quality if you *train* it. It must become *knowing*, it must become critical. Ask it, whenever it wants to spoil something for you, *why* something is ugly, demand proofs from it, test it, and you will find it perplexed and embarrassed perhaps, or perhaps rebellious. But don't give in, insist on arguments and act this way, watchful and consistent, every single time, and the day will arrive when from a destroyer it will become one of your best workers—perhaps the cleverest of all that are building at your life.

Specifically, with respect to the type of sadness I was feeling, he also wrote, "The more still, more patient and more open we are when we are sad, so much the deeper and so much the more will it be *our* destiny." He also likened sadness to a guest that enters a house and forever changes it. The question is, Will we know how? And even if we do become aware, at what level will this awareness take place?

This is important for us spiritually because it is often in the sadness that we make room for God, if, as Rilke suggests, both sides of us are seized. The dream for me awakened a deeper awareness of "the communion of saints"—those people alive and dead who form a community of faith for and within me. I recognized the need not for more and better friends, but for a greater inner awareness of how I could be open to and nurturing of good friendship, even in my recollection of the goodness of those who were now gone. But that was only one side. The other side was the absence of *the* friendship: my relationship with God.

This would take not only an appreciation of God's reflection in others, but also, as Christian Orthodoxy so keenly emphasizes, the presence of God within. Certainly, the gardens where this awareness would grow would be healthy relationships and solitude. Still, in such places, what "doorway" could I enter to appreciate both friendship and alone-time more keenly? Given the premise of this book—the need to *experience* God and life more deeply and intimately—I think one of the best gateways is a deeper appreciation of our emotions and what they can offer us. By putting our "fingers" on the pulse of our emotions, we can be led to look at the cognitions that are giving rise to them as well as our behavior. Furthermore, when we do this with an eye to our relationship with God, our field notes about the ups, downs, and nuances of our daily life become spiritual.

EMOTIONS: THE ROYAL ROAD TO INTIMACY WITH GOD

A spiritual guide related what he felt was a quite sad situation. He had once been speaking to a man who had been a monk for over thirty years. The monk told him that in all those years, he had never really experienced an encounter with God. Oh, he believed in God. There was no question in his mind about that. This monk simply didn't know anything about God that he hadn't learned from a book or someone else.

If I ask people why they feel they have missed God, they express a desire to seek him but are puzzled where to begin or are frustrated at the efforts they have made or are still employing. When I hear such tales, my sense of it is best summed up in a line from an old song "Looking for Love in All the Wrong Places."

God's dramatic initiative to encounter us can neither be taken away nor forced. Yet, as in any relationship, we can do things to appreciate the presence of the other, in this case God. There are many ways we can open ourselves to appreciate God's presence. One key way to ready ourselves every day to welcome God's presence and call to transform our narrative, no matter our stage in life, is to take note of our emotions and ask ourselves how they are leading us to experience God in new ways.

In seeking to appreciate the presence of God through an awareness of our emotions, none should be ignored. Both the positive and what we would term "negative" emotions are portals to experiencing both what God is trying to teach us and ways of intimacy that can only be touched through appreciating those feelings. Emotions serve as hints to look further to see how God may be sitting with us. Let me offer some illustrations.

Recently, I had an opportunity to attend a presentation on St. Teresa of Avila at a Carmelite monastery. During the drive home after the presentation, I realized I had been moved during the event. Even days later, I could still feel a sense of "spiritual intimacy" that I had not experienced in recent days.

As I reviewed the presentation, I thought it was good and I learned several things from the presenter since he was well steeped in Teresian spirituality and history. However, I realized it was not what he said but the spirit within him as he shared his insights. As I reflected further on it, it was also the spirit within the Carmelite community of Sisters and within the persons attending as well. Those with whom we surround ourselves is a key element in our entering the heart of Christ during the day and in our life as a whole. These need not only include people physically present in your life now. They can also be the nourishing support of those whom we may not know or who are no longer living. Through their writings we not only can gain knowledge but also uncover new ways to experience God. They can encourage us to access the other half of our soul— something all of us need desperately in this secular world that wants to fill us with temporal images, food, and values.

SEVERAL SPIRITUAL POINTING FINGERS

Many people, when they pray, *think* of God in ways that make God and their own lives smaller. In prayers of supplication, they may see God as a benevolent corporate CEO. In reviewing their day or life, they may see God as a looming disappointing conscience that only says, "Look at what you have done now!" Or, to the contrary, they may experience God as a "good pal," which may seem nice but certainly drains the splendor of God's wondrous mystery. All of this is based on thought, a projection of one's own images or wishes, but not on the *experience* of God.

In stark contrast to this, John of the Cross's experience of God sits at the center of his life and drives any guidance he offers others. His main, often unstated but felt, goal was to help people believe that the veil between themselves and God was thin or even nonexistent at times. So, for him, rather than "a Sunday God" or a God who could be confined to our image by our own mind, the true God was *everything*. Without a deep desire to make space for God, life became small, meaningless, and frightening for him. With a deep sense of God at the heart of our lives though, we not only seek to make space for encounter but appreciate that in our darkness, God is making new room for himself.

Once again, John's central theme as presented by Iain Matthew:

> John speaks of people who "do not stay empty, so that God might fill them with his ineffable delight; so they leave God just as they came—their hands were already full, and they could not take what God was giving. God saves us from such unhappy burdens which keep us from such fair and wholesome freedom!"
>
> Hands empty and cupped to receive what God is giving: that does evidently depend on John's first word, a self-giving God. Otherwise, space just leaves you with space. *Nada* [nothingness] would be a sad word pronounced on its own. Instead, it is blessed because it

always announces the presence of an "everything being
given in exchange."...The crucial question is not, What
must I achieve? but, what stands in his [God's] way?

In this light, *encounter* with Christ is key in the space we must
earnestly open up and in the space God makes within us. With
such an experience of space within us, we are then positioned as
a nonjudgmental counselor to be a presence to others. John of the
Cross's experience of God led him to help others not to miss their
own opportunity to encounter the holy as well.

Those coming for spiritual direction come with a desire for
God. It is not unusual when we start by asking, "What can I do to meet
God?" and the response is, "You can recognize that in this desire God
is already asking for greater friendship with you." In this appreciation of God's initiative and love, the space we seek to make needs to
be accompanied by a passion for God as central to our lives—not in
imaging a little image of what we think God looks like, but in taking
time in silence and solitude each day to provide the space for God
to sit with us in a personal way, not according to our agenda but as
God wills.

John of the Cross asked us to truly desire and believe that God
at the center of our lives will make life amazing. Even in the darkness, God is not far but journeys with us. It is often in this very darkness that God is making space and offering us new intimacy. We need
to respond by seeking to make space, get out of God's way, and not
settle for less. In a letter to someone he was guiding, John exclaims,
"The person who desires nothing but God does not walk in darkness,
however poor and dark she may be in her own sight."

John of the Cross desperately wants us to believe, not to settle,
and move further and further toward making our life a total joy by
allowing God to fill us in a way that allows us to move toward the
end of our lives with a sense that we have been loved and have loved
others in ways not possible earlier in life. Bede Griffiths, an English
Benedictine priest who went to India, knew this. In his obituary,
The New York Times referred to him as "an entrancing figure...a
man who seemed lost to everything except truth and compassion."
Although intense early in life and not a practicing Christian, he

would eventually reunite with the faith, become Catholic, and then a Benedictine monk. By the time he journeyed to India to found a contemplative community there, he had already become, in the words of his friend Hugh Waterman, "much more now a pervasive light than a consuming flame."

He felt that much of Western Christianity was tied to the intellect. He believed what all Christians needed was to experience more, rather than simply know about, God. In his own life he sought this through periods of meditation and also his deep feeling that we must surrender self-will and be open to the presence and beauty of God all around and within us. Again, from his autobiography *The Golden String*, "I was no longer the centre of my life and therefore I could see God in everything."

He also believed that encountering the spirit of God would be immensely enhanced by the friends that surround you. The company of good people, known in India as *satsang*, would encourage you to experience glimpses of true inner freedom and an attitude that represented a positive undercurrent in your life. In turn, he was a good friend to those he encountered. In the spirit of St. Benedict, he was the perfect guest master. As Shirley duBoulay notes in her biography of him, *Beyond the Darkness*, Bede had the "ability to listen, really to hear what people were saying; in his radical thinking and [his] simple life-style...his openness to new thinking and the way he never, up to the moment of his death, stopped learning." He also had, in the words of Christiane Roper, "real peace, joy and this very lightness of being."

Once again, as in the case of John of the Cross, the message is not that all of us need to live life in such a physically dramatic way. Yet all of us are called to experience God in our own way rather than settle for something less than God. By this I don't mean simply encountering God in quiet prayer or the Eucharist, as important as these are. It must also

- involve the incarnational sense of the Divine in all our thoughts and behavior;
- infuse our attitude and philosophy of life; and

- help us create in ourselves and around us in our interactions with others a place on earth where God can call home.

Such openness to the Divine enables us to partner with God as cocreators in our own formation and in the guidance of the lives of those who surround us.

45 FIELD NOTES FOR PARTNERING WITH GOD

The Divine Presence in and All around Us

With the imagery of the Garden of Eden, we can sense the original blessing of God's pervasive presence in the world. Then, following sin, we experience the absence of God. In Rabbi Abraham Heschel's frame of reference, after original sin, the human person was thrown out of the Garden of Eden. In response, most of humanity built their own "garden" and threw God out. But this was not to remain.

The Jews built a temple as the setting to find and worship God. Then, Jesus came and told his fellow Israelites that if they destroyed that temple, he could rebuild it in three days. By this he obviously was referring to his own resurrection after three days. He was telling them that whereas up to this point they sought God in the temple, now they could find God's presence in him. He would go on later to speak to the disciples about sending the Paraclete when he physically left them. This would mean that then God would be found in the hearts of those who believed in him and followed his example. In this regard, he is speaking about us, who, in partnering with God, become a place to find the Divine and to help others spiritually recognize and reflect the Presence within themselves.

With this in mind, the following field notes on the spiritual life were prepared and are offered to you. They contain the kernels of what I have written before. They represent nothing new. However, they are meant to spiritually and psychologically "dust off" some of the essential elements of living a faithful life of prayer, compassion, deeper self-awareness, and fullness. My hope is that they will stir up not simply thought but also passion and action so you can respond in your own way, with your own gifts, and your own style to create a place that God can call home anew.

I am grateful to Joseph Telushkin's book *Rebbe* on Menachim Schneerson's expounding on Kabalistic teachings concerning divine manifestations throughout the contemporary world.

PRIORITIES

||||||||||||||||||||||||||||||||||||||||||||||||||||||||||||||||||||||||||||||||||||||||||

1. Grace, *Really*

THE UNINTENDED AND OFTEN UNKNOWN POSITIVE IMPACT OF OUR ACTIONS

When I speak to discouraged professional helpers and healers, overwhelmed parents, and harried coworkers, I often hear them sadly relate that they have not succeeded with those they wished to help. In response, in both my presentations and in one-to-one mentoring sessions with them, I think to myself and, if it is appropriate at the time, say to them, "If only you could see how good you are, how gentle you are, and what an important presence you have been to others in this world. If only I could show you a movie of the

47

smiles, small gestures, or unknown positive impacts you have had in so many instances, you would not feel down for very long. You would see God's grace moving through you in unexpected ways and would not give up being a healing presence to others."

I can attest to this in my own life. Recently, for example, I went to speak to almost a thousand people who were marking a year since there had been a mass killing in their city. My goal was to reach out and help them in some way to take the next step in deepening their resilience, increasing their sense of meaning, and strengthening their community given this tragedy.

Whether I succeeded in any way with these goals remains to be seen. Yet the most moving response that encourages me to "continue the good fight" had nothing to do with *my* goals. What one participant wrote in her evaluation that the organizer shared with me was this:

> It's so hard to describe the joy and hope that I felt listening to Dr. Wicks as he spoke even though his talk was on stress and anxiety. My husband, who is recovering from a stroke and has been very depressed, felt his spirit lifted and had many emotional moments listening to Dr. Wicks. He bought one of Dr. Wicks's books *Night Call* and he has a new disposition on his prognosis. I saw his attitude change overnight. Praise God.

Yes, she is right: Praise *God*. I knew it was *grace, really*, not just for her and her husband but for me. As a matter of fact, I sensed being part of a circle of grace in which I was receiving as much, if not more, than I was giving. My hope in sharing this, is that you will, too, especially during those moments when you feel discouraged as a parent, coworker, adult child of an aging parent, or professional helper. To quote Thomas Merton again, "Courage comes and goes... hold on for the next supply!" Both you and others will be grateful if you do.

The woman I quoted above will never know how important her encouragement was and is to me. Let my words be the same for you. Don't give up, especially during these challenging times. You are making a difference even though you may not see it.

|||||||||||||||||||||||||||||||||||||||||||||||||||||||||||||||||||||||||||||||||||||||||||||||||||||||||||||||||||||

2. Hope Grows Here

As I noted in the previous field note, I went to keynote the annual conference of the Diocese of Las Vegas. It was held just prior to the year anniversary of the mass killing at a concert there. Given this, I wondered what the tone would be of the audience of eight hundred that I would speak to on the themes of resilience, self-care, and maintaining a healthy perspective.

When I arrived though, I immediately realized I needn't have worried. The room was filled with great positive energy. The evening program began with rousing music and song. It was also interspersed with photos from the tragedy being posted on large screens. There was also modern dance by two young women portraying the journey from fear, shock, sadness, and death to life and renewed spirit. This was followed up by prayer that interspersed the use of English and Spanish. When I finally got up to speak, I could feel the theme of the conference: *Hope Grows Here.*

From all of this, as well as the energetic reaction to my presentation and the individual comments of persons I met when signing copies of my book *Night Call*, I sensed this event would be a true "circle of grace" for me. I would receive more than I gave. They truly had a sense of what is important because they had learned even more deeply to

- Not shy away, play down, or "spiritualize" the tragedy, hopelessness, depression, and darkness that comes with the sense of sudden, senseless loss that they felt;
- Deepen a sense of community and relationship in which gratitude, compassion, and a better sense of perspective can grow anew—and possibly more deeply after appreciating how precious life is following the killings; and

- Pray more honestly in a way that Paul Tillich's sense of "ecstatic reasoning" (connecting the immediate to the ultimate) allows us to appreciate the meaning in our life in a world marked by narcissism, possessing, divisiveness, unkind speech, and overconcern with image making.

The people in the room with me in Las Vegas had learned that when one is suffering one also must remember the important reality of hope. Hope isn't simply believing because things are going well. Hope is an attitude of living that makes one seek and find new possibilities because of an attitude of trust in God. As Vaclav Havel, the former poet-leader of Czech Republic, once recognized, "Hope is an orientation of the spirit, an orientation of the heart. It is not the conviction that something will turn out well, but the certainty that something makes sense, regardless of how it turns out."

People of true prayer know this and it impacts the hope they are able to embrace, which leads to the compassion by which they are able to live.

3. Let Me Remember

O gentle and caring Spirit of Life,
When I feel frustrated by someone's ingratitude and
seemingly impossible expectations,
let me remember his neediness or fear of saying "Thanks."

When I face a person's rage,
let me remember the pain she has long endured at
the hands of so many others so I can give her the
space to share her anger freely and without fear.

When someone sees the world (and me) in extreme
negative and positive ways,
let me remember that I am neither horrible, nor, for
that matter, am I omnipotent.

When people are very troubled and I begin to feel
    overwhelmed by it all too,
let me remember that "simply listening" is truly a
    quiet, great grace in itself.

And when I see a person making the same mistakes
    over and over again,
let me remember that sometimes I'm not such a
    winner myself!

Yes, as I sit with others who are sad, in pain, under
    stress, depressed, anxious, and afraid, *let me
    remember* the Spirit of gentle faithfulness in this
    world, so I can be present to others the same way
    such a Spirit always is to me.

—Adapted from *After 50* by Robert J. Wicks
(Mahwah, NJ: Paulist Press, 1997)

4. The Amazing Value of Perseverance

A contemporary of Jesus, Rabbi Tarphon, once said, "The day is short, the work is great, the laborers are sluggish, the wages are high, and the Master of the house is insistent. It is not your duty to finish the work, but you are not free to neglect it."

Allen Boesak of South Africa echoed this theme in saying, "We will all go before God to be judged, and God will ask us, 'Where are your wounds?' And we will say, "We have no wounds, Lord.' And God will then ask, 'Was nothing worth fighting for?'"

Yet you may say, "Oh, I don't have to worry about that, I have plenty of wounds to show the Lord!" But I challenge both myself and you, are they real wounds or ones tied to our ego, lack of faith, or failure to appreciate the great virtue of perseverance?

I remember once being invited to speak to a group with terrible morale. Because I am not famous, they didn't know who I was. Yet when I entered the room, I could cut the hate with a knife. I thought, "I'd better give them my best stuff up front" and I did. *Nothing*. I was clinically impressed: I have never seen a group of people keep up hate at such a high pitch for so long.

During the break, I went back to the room they had given me and expressed the wishes of someone with such a big ego as myself who hates to fail. I prayed, "Relieve me of this!" I even went into some Old Testament laments, such as "Smite them and their children," to which I sensed the heavens reply, "I know where you got that, but we don't do that anymore, Bob."

But then as I was sitting there quietly, a piece of Scripture bubbled to the surface that I had read again and again but until this point never fully realized. It was, "They did terrible things to me and the prophets before me. They will do the same and worse to you at times." What I sensed the Lord was telling me was this: "Normally when you say religious things, people smile and they hug you, but when things get difficult, you want to run away."

Even when things are not that troublesome, we want to deny, avoid, or escape. Staying in place during difficult times is no longer seen as something expected of us. Perseverance is something that is a scarce commodity today. Because of this, I wonder whether it has lost its value for most young people. Yet when I read the following story, which I will close this reflection with, I was reminded of its value.

Even though I was a U.S. Marine Corps officer, I don't think of it much. Too many of my fellow marines truly suffered and I didn't, so although I wore the uniform, I know that the true heroes didn't include me. However, the following story brought me back to the days when I was in training and taught the value of perseverance. It is the same perseverance to which most spiritual philosophies and faiths ascribe to as worth emulating.

As I said, I don't know the source of the following brief story, but it certainly makes the point I want to share:

A nurse took the tired, anxious serviceman to the bedside.

"Your son is here," she said to the old man lying in

the hospital bed. She had to repeat the words several times before the patient's eyes opened. Heavily sedated because of the pain of his heart attack, he dimly saw the uniformed Marine standing just outside the oxygen tent. He reached out his hand. In turn, the Marine wrapped his toughened fingers around the old man's limp ones, squeezing a message of love and encouragement.

The nurse brought a chair so that the Marine could sit beside the bed. All through the night the young Marine sat there in the poorly lit ward, holding onto the old man's hand to offer him a sense of love and strength. Occasionally, the nurse suggested to the Marine that he move away and rest awhile. He refused.

Whenever the nurse came onto the ward, the Marine was oblivious of her and the night noises of the hospital—the clanking of the oxygen tank, the laughter of the night staff members exchanging greetings, the cries and moans of other patients. Now and then she heard him say a few gentle words. The dying man said nothing, only held tightly his son's hand all through the night.

Along toward dawn, the old man died. The Marine then released the now lifeless hand he had been holding all night and went to tell the nurse. While she did what she needed to do, he waited.

Finally, she returned and started to offer words of sympathy, but the Marine interrupted her with the question, "Who was that man?"

The nurse was startled. "Why, he was your father," she answered.

"No, he wasn't," calmly replied the Marine. "I never saw him before in my life."

"Then why didn't you say something when I took you to him?"

"I knew right away there had been a mistake, but I also knew he needed his son, and his son just wasn't here for him. When I realized that he was too sick to tell whether or not I was his son, knowing how much he needed me to be him, I stayed."

The lesson? The next time someone needs you, just be there. *Stay.*

||||||||||||||||||||||||||||||||||||||||||||||||||||||||||||||||||||||||||||||||||||||||||

5. Love, Naturally

On one of my trips to Thailand to present to caregivers, relief workers, and NGOs (nongovernmental organizations), I visited a refugee center operated there by the Maryknoll Fathers, Brothers, and Sisters. As I was sitting in one of the offices with the priest who was its director, a man with a wide-eyed stare appeared at the window and just as quickly disappeared. When I gave the priest a quizzical look as to what that was about, he smiled in return.

He then told me that the person who just appeared was referred to by the Thai staff as being "not full." Because the priest was a clinician himself when this man arrived at the refugee center with such great problems, he asked the staff at a meeting, "What can we possibly do with him?"

He said, "In return, they looked puzzled, stared at each other for a moment, and then one of them quietly said, "Why, love him of course."

He told me at that moment he was so proud of them, he was speechless. He could only beam with joy at their compassionate attitude.

As we face the sometimes seemingly insurmountable problems of contemporary society filled with such anger and divisiveness as well as the physical, economic, and psychological issues confronting some in our family and circle of friends, we might recall the simple role that true religion and spirituality calls all of us to: *Why, love him, of course*. It is an attitude and approach that we must own and act upon in the unique way each of us is able to do. Anything less is not reflective of any true religion or spirituality. It needs to start with us and when we stop being judgmental of others who may not seem to be behaving the way we want, it is a great beginning. I know that is a good attitude for me to embrace more fully, especially now and in the days to come.

||||||||||||||||||||||||||||||||||||||||||||||||||||||||||||||||||||||||||||||||||||||||||||||

6. A Surprising Secret

Years ago, I came across what I felt was a surprising secret to living a rich, full, and balanced life. It was shared many, many years ago and sat there in full sight. I knew the key for me was to truly take it to heart and follow where it might lead me at each stage of my life.

When I speak to groups, I often mention it at the beginning of my presentations. I lead into what I am about to share with them with the recognition that all of us need a mentor. The mentor can be real or "virtual." In other words, we learn from this type of person through their writings or the guidance from them that others have recorded.

After this prelude, I tell them I am going to share a story from my primary mentor and tradition. I then suggest to them that no matter what faith, philosophy, or psychology they may follow that they consider the guidance I offer them from the Christian tradition. If they don't follow this faith, they should then look to their own belief system or philosophy of life to see what their own guides also have suggested in their writings or in person about what I suggest.

With this said as a backdrop, I indicate that I am going to share a question Jesus was asked and how he responded in Matthew 22:34–40. The question asked was one that rabbis, not simply Jesus, were asked all the time: What is the greatest commandment? To this he responded like any other good rabbi would in the following two ways. First, he set the people at ease in how he initially responded, and then he pulled the rug out from under them to wake them up. Second, like other rabbis, he reached into Torah for his answer.

To answer he selected from Leviticus and Deuteronomy by initially choosing a "heavy" precept from the 613 precepts of the Pharisees of the day when he said, "You must love God with your whole heart and your whole mind and your whole soul." In our minds, we can visualize the Jews present nodding their heads in assent. After all, how could you disagree with this if you were a faithful Jew?

But then he reached down and selected a light precept and held it up on the same level as the heavy one and said, "And, you must love your neighbor as yourself." In focusing on the neighbor, he was following the spirit of the Book of Exodus where we read that Moses is told by God that the Israelites must not simply find God vertically in prayer but also horizontally through each other.

Let me take a moment to unpack this a bit. I believe that Jesus was teaching his listeners and us that being compassionate with others is an essential linchpin of a truly meaningful and rewarding life. As author Henry James once quipped, "Get out of yourself and stay out."

However, presence to others is intimately linked with presence to self because you can't share what you don't have. Therefore, self-care, self-understanding, and self-love are not simply about us.

So, what Jesus is saying very clearly is that we need a *balance* of presence to others, self, and God. The question for us today is this: How are we in balance with being present simultaneously to others, self, and God?

With respect to *presence to others*, some say to me, "What can I do for others? I am not in the helping, healing business?" I respond by indicating to them that a listening presence alone is healing. Others are too busy with seeking to enjoy their own lives and think little of others. I still remember playing tennis years ago when visiting a friend who lived in a gated community. On the next court the two men playing kept trying to top each other with their plans for vacations, places to go out to eat, and shows they would see. It is great to enjoy yourself, but if that is the only interest you have and no time is spent thinking of and helping others, it seems sad somehow. On a very basic level, life isn't as much fun when we don't reach out but stay in the narrow cocoon of inordinate self-interest. Focus solely on pleasure for yourself and you will miss out on joy.

Presence to self, on the other hand, is also important. Yet it is frequently ignored by persons who wish to be a compassionate presence to others. This is also sad because compassion should include self-compassion. Once again, you can't share what you don't have, so even when you are present to yourself in a healthy way, it is really not all about you. Presence to self needs to include a healthy, creative, and ambitious as well as realistic self-care protocol or program. (If you wish to read more on this, check out my book *Bounce: Living a Resilient Life* in your library.). All too often, we psychologically or spiritually nourish ourselves with whatever comes along. I think the humorist Erma Bombeck was onto something when she teased, "I think that any man that watches 3 football games in a row should be declared legally dead!" The question that is important for you if you wish to remain resilient is, What are you nourishing yourself with now—and yes, including watching a couple of football games now and then is fine.

Finally, *presence to God* is the most essential element in the balance equation. For Christians, I suggest that they strengthen their "rule of prayer" so they include such elements as liturgy, formal prayer, conversations with God, faith sharing, Scripture, spiritual reading, informal journaling at day's end, music, spiritual direction, spiritual friendship, and "alone-time" (time spent in silence and solitude or being reflective when in a group).

The last element is the most essential for me. I need to take at least a few moments in silence and solitude and wrapped in gratitude each day. People say to me, "I just don't have the time." My response to them is to offer Stephen Covey's suggestion that we must not simply prioritize our schedule but actually schedule our priorities. I also add that they can start by using the "crumbs of alone-time and mindfulness" that already exist in their schedule, such as the few moments you are awake before getting out of bed in the morning, during a shower, while taking a walk during lunchtime, in the drive home without the radio on, and so on.

A simple prayer at night before going to bed also helps us keep life in balance with God at its center and is especially necessary during tough days and times in life. Given this, I think what God would say (if present here and now) to those committed to living a compassionate, rich life is contained in the refrain from David Haas's well-known and loved song "You Are Mine." I think what God would say to you, good people, *especially* in your toughest moments, is

Do not be afraid. I am with you.
I have called you each by name.

Come follow me, I will bring you home.
I love you...you are mine. (Based on Isa 43:1)

||||||||||||||||||||||||||||||||||||||||||||||||||||||||||||||||||||||||||||||||||||||||||||||||

7. Silent Listening Is Usually the Best Course of Action—but Not Always!

Several months ago, a friend surprised me when she said, "I don't like the pope." When I asked her why, because I admire the pope's gentle courage and faithfulness to the gospel, she responded, "I think he should stay out of politics and stick to religion." I knew by the way she said this with such emphasis that she also meant, sticking to the type of religion that *didn't offer any new challenges to change her own views or behavior.*

In response, I remained silent, feeling whatever I might say at the moment would only just aggravate her and not accomplish very much. Maybe I was right because psychological and spiritual guides need to be careful in the phrasing and timing of their interventions. In the delicate work with persons suffering—sometimes because the patients or clients are unconsciously contributing to the problem themselves by how they are thinking or behaving—therapists and spiritual mentors must learn to

- Tell people what they don't like,
- In ways they can best hear it,
- At a time when they are most able to accept it.

However, having said that, if I would be in a position like that again, I might still say, "Well, Jesus got involved in politics when he delivered the Sermon on the Mount. I guess the pope is just following his example."

We must carefully judge what our real intention is though when we are intervening at certain times with the people around us. Is it just to make ourselves feel better by getting something off our chest, or do we feel that we are actually being called at that moment to share what we truly believe and then let God take care of the residue?

58

I still feel that listening to others and offering them the space to express themselves without fear of judgment, reprisal, or an immediate reaction is a great gift. People count on us to do a "double reflection" when they share something negative, outrageous, or emotionally laden. By a "double reflection" I mean that rather than let someone trigger an unhelpful immediate reaction from us like other people in their lives might, it is important that we reflect within ourselves about why we are having a certain response to what was said *before* reflecting with them on the issue.

When we do this we may recognize that the timing may not be right when the other person is upset to offer a contrary position for them to consider. Also, we may be too upset to provide a helpful response at the moment. This is so because when we are caught off guard by something we believe to be wrong or negative, we may emotionally respond in-kind, and this does little to help the person consider another view.

However, I am also aware that many people, myself included, often don't say anything because of a lack of courage or a fear of rejection. Therefore, I also try to keep in mind Nelson Mandela's wise caution: "Fools multiply when wise persons are silent."

Bottom line: Silent listening is usually the best course of action...*but not always!*

8. Above All, Take Yourself Lightly

One of the sad trends that I see in American life today is the inability to take oneself lightly. It seems that many stars in entertainment and sports as well as contemporary leaders in politics, education, and even organized religion have a hard time laughing at themselves.

Inflating ourselves is a problem for all of us in life. That is why I was interested in what a famous statesman would say when he was asked why the politics in education were so nasty. His simple answer: "Because the stakes are so low."

When situations bring out the haughtiness and inflated ego in me, I turn to the words of persons who are close to power, know the stress of it, and realize how important it is to have a sense of humor to survive: namely, the *mothers of U.S. presidents*.

The two who come to mind immediately are Lillian Carter, the mother of President Jimmy Carter, and Barbara Bush, the wife of President George H. W. Bush and the mother of President George W. Bush. Once when Mrs. Carter was asked if she ever got discouraged, she nodded affirmatively and replied, "Sometimes I look around at my children and think, I should have remained a virgin!"

On Barbara Bush's last hospital stay before she died, she was sitting with her nurse and in walked her son George. When this happened she turned to the nurse, pointed at her son, the former president of the United States, and asked, "Do you know why he is the way he is?" When the nurse, surprised by the question, shook her head, Mrs. Bush answered, "Because I smoked and drank when I was pregnant with him."

My style is fairly intense and being passionate I think has allowed me to do some good things in my life when the odds against me were fairly high. However, we can lose our way when we care and instead of taking the mission seriously we take an unfortunate detour at times and take ourselves too seriously instead. This is not only harmful for us but also can be problematic for those who work with us.

Having a sense of humor can allow us to roll more freely with failure, adversity, and defeat. It also can help us pick our battles more carefully so that we don't burn out. A Jesuit priest I know wryly commented to me when he saw how seriously I was taking too many things: "Please remember, Bob, Jesus only got crucified *once*! Everything is not worth the intensity you are giving it."

My father-in-law had another response to me in such situations. When he saw the look on my face about something I was getting all worked up about, he would say, "Be careful your face doesn't freeze like that."

Even people who admit they don't have a natural sense of humor or inclination to be able to tease or laugh at themselves in a gentle way, can do things to help alleviate their tendency toward unnecessary glumness and the brittleness of worry.

Once, a student at the beginning of a three-week summer

course said she didn't have much of a sense of humor, and asked me what she might do since she had a hard time lightening up. I told her that when she felt like this she should go home, get under the kitchen table, and sing a song loudly. She said, and she didn't mean this as a pun, "You're not serious!" I responded that I was.

For some reason, I didn't ask her during the next class whether she did it or not. However, on the last day of the course, I finally did. In response, she smiled and said, "Yes, I did...but not before I closed all the shades on the windows because I was afraid someone would see me doing it!" She, along with the rest of the class, laughed loudly.

I did see her again after about a year. And, yes, when I saw her, there was still a big smile on her face. I must confess that I almost didn't recognize her. She had crossed the Rubicon of knowing she could be silly as a way of breaking the back of grimness.

Do whatever it takes to be able to gently laugh at yourself, tease yourself about having such a big ego, and seek to take yourself more lightly. I think it will not only help you but those you interact with who need your "lightness" at times when they are feeling so heavy. It doesn't mean that you don't care. To the contrary, it signifies that you care so much that you don't want to lose your way in the process of reaching out to others in need.

9. A Piece of Desert Wisdom for Modern Life

As many know from their church history, when Emperor Constantine declared in the fourth century that Christianity was no longer an outlaw religion, it upset certain people. They were worried that with this move, the Church would no longer be a countercultural force. They were concerned the Church would become simply another secular institution with no real prophetic voice. It would become domesticated.

As a result, many women and men fled to the desert, which, as we know and image, is a physically dry, barren desolate area, usually covered with sand, waterless, and with little, if any, vegetation. Some of the people who went didn't fare too well because they did it as an "ego-trip" and were there only to be alone with themselves and listen to their own voice. (We can see that problem today with some figures desiring to return to the religion of the nineteenth century.)

Others, however, who became known as desert *Ammas* (mothers) and *Abbas* (fathers), were there to be alone with God. The silence and solitude were present so they could hear the voice of God more clearly. From books on these saintly figures by such writers as Benedicta Ward, Thomas Merton, Henri Nouwen, and Douglas Christie (as well as my own little work *Crossing the Desert*), we can see the holiness reflected in the sayings of these role models in saintliness.

Today, we may disregard such individuals from the fourth century as being overly "saintly" and too far from the realm that we live in now. However, as minimalist poet Robert Lax noted in a letter to one of his friends, "The saints are examples of attainable virtue, not a show of divine freaks." The Ammas and Abbas moved to the desert so they might be free of not only what would keep them from an intimate relationship with God but also to release them from anything that would prevent a gentle understanding and embrace of others—a lesson that many people, myself included, sometimes forget.

Earlier in my life, for example, I spent more time on being judgmental: "She's on her knees at daily Mass but then leaves and is nasty to others....He says he is 'religious' but doesn't offer money to those in need....She visits the food pantry for free meals but spends what money she has on alcohol and cigarettes." Now, as I age, I feel differently.

I now think it is good that the person on her knees is at least trying to be faithful and is often nasty out of fear. The person who is "religious" but gives little of their wealth is ignorant of all of God's calling to share with the less fortunate and may still learn to be truly generous. The person who drinks, smokes, and then seeks governmental or local handouts has probably had a truly hard life and the drink and smoke are the only "friends" he or she presently has to make life a bit easier and more enjoyable. One of the main fruits of desert wisdom is to have us take a step back from being quick to judge others. Instead, if we lean back in reflection it is to ask forgiveness for our own sins instead.

But how did the Ammas and Abbas come to realizations like this? What can we do to prevent our faith from becoming domesticated or our attitude toward others so judgmental?

One of the key ways they embraced the grace of a good attitude is by developing their own "rule of prayer," which freed them from being dominated by *chronos*, secular values and personal negative or judgmental impulses. Instead, the rule of prayer that they developed in entering the desert opened them up to live more gently and compassionately by embracing *kairos*, God's values, instead.

The rule of prayer was made up of many things but often included *liturgy*, where they could meet God in the Word, the Eucharist, and each other; *formal prayer*, like the psalms; *silent mental conversations with God*; and *reflections during the day*, because someone once said that life is something that often happens while we are busy doing something else. Their rule of prayer also included *spiritual reading, especially Sacred Scripture*, where our identity is on the line (theologian Karl Barth once noted that when we read the Bible and ask, What is this book saying? it should respond, Who is it that is asking?). In addition, *faith sharing* with others, *acts of compassion*, and *contemplation or meditation* are also part of what the desert fathers and mothers embraced to allow prayer to drive their lives.

If we already have these elements of prayer in our life, the question then becomes, How can we emphasize those areas of our rule of prayer to which we give little attention? We can also ask, "How can we deepen the aspect of our rule of prayer that we already love and find renewing?" For example, if we love to meditate in church before the Eucharist, we might consider reading something about the theology of the Eucharist. If we find our relationship with Mary, the mother of Jesus, is important to us, we should seek out a sound book about current, rather than overly pietistic, Marian theology and spirituality. In a similar vein, if we love to meditate, maybe we should seek a spiritual guide to help us go deeper. This is done so the aspects of our prayer life remain dynamic, encouraging, and challenging. Otherwise, they run the risk of simply turning into idols or mental places to hide.

Today, more than ever, we need to embrace the spiritual desert within contemporary society and live in it in a way that our relationship with God becomes deeper and our compassion more understanding. Otherwise, our religion will simply take its place alongside culture, politics, and economics. We will only be interested in preserving our little world while we ignore the greater spiritual calling to spend the brief time we have left on this earth by embracing inner peace and joy as well as being compassionate enough to understand the plight of others and understanding enough to *be a bit kinder*.

IDENTITY

10. Uncover Real Goodness to See the Complete Truth about Society—and *Yourself*

As I listened carefully to a psychologist-patient of mine berate herself for things she had done wrong, I motioned that I wanted to say something. When she responded by stopping her self-blaming litany, I asked, "Why do you think it is that you often hear praise in a whisper and negative feedback as thunder?"

The same can be said of society today. On the Web, in newspapers, and on television we often read or hear what is wrong with the world, America, and our communities today. While the comments made are usually factually accurate, they are only part of the story of what is going on around us. Just as the psychologist I just mentioned kept the reality of her gifts and generosity seemingly at bay while she focused solely on her failings, so does the rumor mill and the media with respect to current events. The simple reality is that bad stories sell papers, while good stories often go underreported.

Yet occasionally an article is published or story is shared that counterculturally brings to the fore the basic goodness that is at the heart of most people and societies. We then see that even when there is darkness, there is also light.

One such report was a recent one by Sandra Garcia for *The New York Times*. In the article she wrote that a two-year-old boy's parents were informed five weeks earlier that he had a rare form of brain cancer. In his case this meant that he only had two months left in his young life. Already, the frenetic energy that marks the toddler stage was gone from him, as was the use of his left arm and leg.

In response, since they knew their child would not live to see another Christmas, they decided to celebrate the season early for him by putting up a lighted tree and decorating their home. He wouldn't know it was not really Christmas, and they felt he could truly enjoy the decorations and spirit of the season before he died.

Because he also liked to sit outside in his red flyer wagon bundled up in a hoodie and blanket, the neighbor also decided to decorate so he could have the fun of seeing inflatable toys in her yard. Another neighbor, who only speaks Spanish, somehow learned about the little boy's plight as well and also decorated outside. The neighborhood even went on to schedule a Christmas parade later in the month for him.

As you can imagine, the parents were totally distraught over their son's impending death. However, the child's mother, while noting how difficult it was in knowing her son would soon be gone, said about him upon seeing his wonderful reactions to the decorations, "It is really hard, but I love seeing the joy in his eyes." The first important lesson in this story is that communities often have more good than bad in them. The love is there if we look for it, and we must.

The second lesson is a more personal one for each of us. As I mentioned at the beginning of this reflection, I also feel a similar reaction to a much, much less dire situation when I deal with individuals who are not dying but are in a downward negative spiral.

When I lecture, mentor, and conduct therapy—especially with helpers and healers such as educators, psychotherapists, nurses, physicians, social workers, members of the military, and persons in
full-time ministry—I can often see the sadness in their eyes as they
speak about themselves. The paradox is that they seem so hard on
themselves even though they are doing so much good.

I often see the same in parents, adult children caring for their
elders, and compassionate coworkers. When this occurs, I must confess that I also experience a degree of sadness myself as well as a
degree of puzzlement. At that point I think to myself, "If only you
could see how good you are. If only you could feel what a positive
difference you have gently made in so many people's lives." My hope
then is at some point in our time together that they will once again
be able to regain perspective and see themselves through the loving
eyes of God. In sharing this, I would like you to know that is also my
hope for you.

What I am suggesting is not a journey in glossing over personal
mistakes and just being "nice." No. It is not an interior pilgrimage in
spiritual or psychological romanticism and denial. That helps no one.

Instead, it is a deep belief that while we need to be clear about
our growing edges, there is nothing to be gained by looking at our
sins *exclusively*. Alongside a sound awareness of our failings, we must
simultaneously view our gifts and the love of God for us. Otherwise,
just like the news reports that highlight only the sad occurrences of
life (even though they be true), our personal assessment will be mis-
directed and quite incomplete. However, when we can see our signature strengths and gifts as clearly as our faults, we are then in a good
position to uncover and nourish more of our talents. This will allow us
to have a more accurate picture of what we have to enjoy and share.
Knowing our gifts can also provide greater strength and impetus to
deal with our weaknesses. When this occurs, we will feel more satisfaction with our lives. As a result, we will be in a much better position
to help others as well as have a greater sensitivity to all the goodness
that is already around and within us that we may be missing.

It is worth searching for the good that is truly there. As a matter of fact, in these often difficult times, it is not a nicety, it is a necessity. Happy hunting!

11. A Simple Expression of Self

Once we are in our forties, I think there is an important spiritual desire: to have a simple expression of self. We wish to be an integrated person without guile who can purify the world a bit through honesty, transparency, and a willingness to be a person for others. This is especially so in times like today when narcissism and the desire to have or be more are so prevalent.

As I was reflecting on the sixth chapter of John's Gospel this morning, I read a line and had to burst out laughing. It was written, "When Jesus realized that they were about to come and make him king, he withdrew again to the mountain by himself." I thought what leading figure in professional sports, entertainment, or (especially) politics would do this today? Instead, at the very least some would reply instead, "What a good idea to make me king!"

Because God, not the world, has a copyright on our identity and the way it is manifested at each phase of our life, the question I think we need to ask ourselves is, What would be a simple expression of self for us that would be genuine and encourage others to be authentic as well?

The question is a basic but not easy one—at least not for me. When I think of it at this point in my life, the words *kindness* and *gentleness* seem to be the answer for me to become more authentic and helpful to others. Yet many times when I focus on kindness as a way of expressing a simple sense of self, I recall how unkind I have been at times in my life. When I seek to be gentle, I also fail a great deal, which sometimes leads to a sense of discouragement with respect to my chances of success in the future.

But success alone is the draw of self-help books that are limited to attracting people who want something for themselves, not those who want to reach out with compassion to others as well. It is faithfulness to finding a simple expression of self that is transformative. This is so because through a simple expression of the true self we experience our limits, our need for grace, our failure when we seek to go it alone without helpful companions, and our sense of humility.

People who know me are usually aware of two things: (1) I get too filled up with my own importance and big ego at times; and (2) I believe that humility is essential to seek even if we often don't find it, because when you take knowledge and you add humility, you get wisdom. When you take that very wisdom and add it to compassion, you get love, and at the heart of life is love: God is love.

So, what is your simple sense of self now? Knowing and expressing it, even if you fail a lot like me, can help in these times when people are tempted to say things that belittle, divide, and deprive those who most need their encouragement. Seeking your simple sense of self is an act of prayer because you are seeking to be the whole person God wishes you to be and then share it with others in need.

12. The Four Necessary Friends

Recently, I offered morning presentations on resilience to the membership of the International Civilian Aviation Chaplains. What a great group of committed professionals. Directly from that presentation in North Carolina, I flew to Las Vegas to speak again on resilience and self-care. It was about a year after they experienced a mass killing at a concert there. In preparing both presentations I realized one of the themes that is particularly important for me to remember when guiding people to enhance personal and professional hardiness is *friendship*.

As I get older, the importance of having a well-rounded circle of good friends becomes clearer. I truly agree with the Cameroonian proverb: "If you want to go fast, go alone. If you want to go far, go together." However, even though parents, teachers, and other types of mentors advise us that we should select our friends carefully, they rarely expand on this as to what *type* of friends would be important voices of encouragement to living a full and meaningful life. In response, I would like to take a stab at offering some suggestions.

My sense is that we need four specific types of persons in our circle of friends if we are going to make it and, more than that, have a life that continues to include "unlearning" and new learning, enough support, the ability to learn to laugh at ourselves, and to be inspired again and again.

The first type of friend no one really likes. Henry David Thoreau once quipped, "If you see someone coming to do good for you...run for your life!" This type of friend is the *prophet*. No one likes the prophet, but we need this type of individual to wake us up from time to time. If we feel we are totally free, we are lost. At each stage of life there are "invisible puppeteers" that arise from our unconscious, past, or old unexamined erroneous beliefs (hidden schemata) that surface to hold us back. To counteract this natural movement away from the truth and growth for each of us is the prophet who asks, "What voices are guiding you? What voices are silently leading you in a direction that is not helpful?"

Balancing the prophet is another important type of friend: the *cheerleader*. So, who is the cheerleader? The cheerleader is the person who is sympathetic and will offer a soothing spirit no matter what. Our cheerleaders are very important because they reflect the loving face of God. From them we learn what *imago Dei*, being made in the image and likeness of God, really means.

If you only have prophets in your life, you will burn out or at the very least become unnecessarily discouraged. Whereas, if you only have cheerleaders, you won't grow. (You can see this especially in narcissistic leaders who are not open to criticism or correction but become explosively angry and defensive instead of willing to learn and change.) When I work with new psychotherapists, counselors, spiritual directors, educators, mentors, and parents, I ask them to balance the prophetic with the supportive, clarity with kindness. With too much clarity, we can hurt people to the core (cause "narcissistic injury"); with too much kindness, there is no growth.

The third type of friend is the *harasser* or *teaser*. This person is necessary because on the way to taking faith, family, and friends seriously, we run the danger of sometimes taking a detour that results in taking ourselves too seriously. This can be dangerous not only to us but to those around us. It is akin to becoming like a brittle tree that when the winds of change blow through it—as they always will—we will break. When this happens not only will it hurt us but the "broken branches" of our upset may fall on those around us as well. Harassers keep us from taking ourselves so seriously and help us to laugh at a certain person: *ourselves*. This enables us to keep things in perspective, even during the hard, sensitive, and stressful times. What a gift such persons are to us and the world.

Finally, we also need a friend who is *inspirational*. This individual is the one who is able to call us to be all we can be without embarrassing us because we are where we are at any given point in time. We may find such persons in a mentor, wiser colleague, spiritual guide, spiritual director, counselor, or therapist, or even in the writings of someone we respect and want to emulate. This is, indeed, a rare individual but you will know when you have encountered one. For example, Matthieu Ricard, in his widely read book *Happiness*, wrote, "Everything changed when I met a few remarkable beings who exemplified what a fulfilling life can be." In a similar vein, Steve Georgiou wrote in his book *Way of the Dreamcatcher* about the minimalist poet and best friend of Thomas Merton, Robert Lax: "I remember how after spending long evenings with Lax, I would leave his hermitage and feel as if I had landed on the earth for the first time."

Therefore, I believe the four types of friends who are necessary for a rich, balanced, and committed life are the prophet, the cheerleader, the harasser or teaser, and the inspirational friend. Accordingly, I believe it would be helpful if we asked, Who are these people or "voices" (because sometimes certain people can play different multiple roles) in our life?

A well-rounded circle of friends is not something to take for granted, especially if we really want to live the rest of our days in a rich and compassionate way. As Reinhold Niebuhr, American theologian, ethicist, and commentator on politics and public affairs, aptly noted, "Nothing we do, no matter how virtuous, can be accomplished alone." Amen.

Good luck on uncovering and benefitting from such friends. Remember, they may be hiding in plain sight.

|||||||||||||||||||||||||||||||||||||||||||||||||||||||||||||||||||||||||||||||||||||||||||

13. The Three Journeys All of Us Must Take

The first inner journey is the most straightforward. It also takes up more than half our life. It is the journey to find our true "name."

People see us in many ways, but God has the copyright on our true charism, our central gift in life. It is the one that we are called to fully enjoy and share freely with others. In my own case, I have found *passion* to be the word that most fully describes who I am at the core of my personality.

This first inner journey in self-understanding usually takes more than half our life until we realize that we are being called to a second journey. It is one in which our attention is more drawn to how we can "prune" our primary charism through embracing a second word or name. In my case, I found that at a point in my forties and fifties, my gift of passion needed balancing or pacing in its delivery. When I felt anxious, my passion (ego) would fill the room. In an effort to be passionate with others, sometimes I would be intrusive instead of encouraging, which was not very helpful. So, the second journey for me was to embrace gentleness so I could live a gentle passionate life—to be, if you will, com*passion*ate. If your word or name is *listener*, for instance, then maybe in your forties and fifties you would be called to embrace *assertive* as your other word, so that you become an assertive listener. It differs from person to person, from charism to charism, as to what the pruning or balancing word would be depending upon what your central gift is.

The third journey is the most mysterious of all, and generally we are asked to take it in our fifties, sixties, or even later. The best way to describe it is by way of a story. A spiritual traveler in his mid-fifties visited a mentor who knew him well. When she asked him how he was progressing spiritually, he humbly said, "Step by little step." To that the mentor smiled and said, "That will no longer be good enough. You can't cross a spiritual canyon by taking small steps. At this point, instead you must leap into the darkness."

That spiritual and psychological leap is when we are called to take the second "word" or "name" we have chosen and make it our central focus, our first name. In my case, it meant that instead of being passionate in the best way possible, I needed to focus on being gentle. If it is done correctly, people won't really notice. In my case, they should always see me as passionate in some way. However, without being aware of it, they should leave me and experience the gentleness in some way if I am truly centered on it.

Now, why is this third journey *a leap into the darkness*? In my case, when I felt I was being called to emphasize gentleness and shone a psychological light on this trait, I could see how many times I had failed in this regard in the past. Moreover, even when I tried to turn over a new leaf and be a gentler person in the present, I would often fail and feel this failure to reach my goal in a deeply moving way.

You might reasonably ask, Then why would you continue to do this when you could simply go back to being passionate in the best way possible? Because in responding to the call to take the third journey, I began to feel a new sense of freedom and understanding of the reality of Grace. I began to realize at a new level that I could not do it by myself. Instead, I needed to embrace the Ignatian theme: Work as if it were all in your hands while recognizing it is all in God's hands. Furthermore, by emphasizing a lesser gift, my eyes began to open to see more clearly the other signature strengths God had given me that I was unable to see while I was in control. Up to this point, the primary light of my personality had been blinding me to the "lesser" gifts God had given me to enjoy and share freely. Quite a gift when you think about it.

The spiritual journey to respond to God's call, especially later in life, is not easy though. Abram could have simply stayed comfortable, but instead he responded to the call to be Abraham, the father of his people. His wife, Sarai, could have given up her desire to be a mother so late in life, but she responded as well to become Sarah, a woman filled with new potential.

What will your response be when you are called to embrace an identity copyrighted by God and not the world? Those who love you and a world that needs you to be all that you are called to be are waiting to see your response.

‖‖

14. A Puzzling, Lonely Moment Potentially Filled with Great Rewards

Sometimes we are completely caught off guard by a feeling of psychologically and spiritually bone-chilling loneliness. It can happen at the strangest of moments. Possibly it occurs when you are sitting with a wonderful group of people and suddenly a sense of alienation envelopes you and you think, "These are terrific people. Many are my friends. Yet I feel different, cut off, separate from them."

Maybe it is on a tennis court. You can't help but overhear the two players on the other court comparing notes as to their last vacation abroad. You are trying to focus on the game, not eavesdropping on them, but are then struck with the thought, "Is that all that interests you in life? Is this what it is all about—whose vacation is more impressive?" Then you catch yourself being judgmental, but it doesn't keep you from feeling you just don't belong. As one patient told me, "I think what I am meant to be in life is a lighthouse attendant."

Possibly you were walking through a beautiful countryside. As you walked, you noticed a herd of deer in the distance and a red fox racing by just beyond the barbed-wire fence that was encircling a group of cows grazing in the pasture. As you did this, you remembered a criticism from someone about how you behaved yesterday at lunch and thought, "I feel closer and more at ease in nature than with people. I let my hair down with people and rather than them sensing my trust in the relationship, they take offense at my comments and fail to think beyond the words to my intention. I feel more comfortable here."

Or, maybe a positive event produces the feeling of loneliness. Someone sitting next to you on a plane gets into a conversation about something with you and there is a feeling of genuine connection. You will never see this person again, yet he seems to "get you" and be able to explore the aspects of your journey in life that childhood friends don't. Then, after it is over and you are deplaning, you experience that sense of loneliness...but as in the other instances, the story doesn't end there.

Instead, in each instance it is actually the beginning of a transforming experience. It awakens in you to the sense of your own uniqueness in the eyes of God. *Only God* will ever really, completely "get you." You remember at that moment of loneliness and separation that you are not really, totally alone or on your own. You feel at the core of your existence that your name is written in the palm of his hand. You recall the messages from John's Gospel: "I won't leave you orphaned; I will come back for you....You are my friend." You are not really alone.

It's a shame that periods of loneliness are often not unwrapped for what they can be: a chance to go spiritually deeper and to be a gentler, understanding presence to others when they are having a tough time in their own journey because of experiences of feeling apart. Worth praying over, I think.

15. Biographies of Life—*Our* Life

Early in life we were probably attracted to reading biographies of persons who are actualized versions of who we believe we are. This is good because they inspire us to truly develop the gifts we have been given, which make up our unique sense of self. If you are a passionate person like I am, you seek out those who have not settled for a safe existence but wanted to be part of something greater. It is very exciting.

Then, later on, you seek wisdom figures who will provide the wisdom to live a deeper life, while still maintaining the style for which you are known and that people count on. For me, one such book like that today is *Rebbe*, the life and teachings of Menachem M. Schneerson, by Joseph Telushkin. This towering leader of the Chabad-Lubavitch movement inspired me as a Christian to create a place God could call home on this earth, to be a partner with God.

According to Telushkin, "The Rebbe came with a different message, one that he preached for over forty years: Love your fellow, and not just those who agree with you." In addition, he sought a true embrace of the entire Jewish people. As former British chief rabbi Jonathan Saks pointed out about Schneerson, "If the Nazis searched out every Jew in hate, the Rebbe wished to search out every Jew in love." Such a passion for what is good! This biography touched me to the core.

However, it is my belief that later in life, we need to not only read biographies of persons who model who we wish to be in terms of our central *charism*, or gift. We need to read biographies of persons who represent our "shadow"—in other words, that primary talent that would balance and bring out the richness of our major gift even more. For me, this meant seeking out a biography of a person who was known for her or his spirit of "gentleness."

I initially discovered such gentleness in a brief work on the minimalist poet Robert Lax, who was also contemplative Thomas Merton's best friend since their college years at Columbia. A simple moving book by Steve Georgiou, *Way of the Dreamcatcher*, whet my initial desire to experience a person who was marked by simplicity, humility, transparency, and had a keen ability to truly listen, not simply wait for his opportunity to speak. Then, I wished for a more major work on Lax and his life but I knew of none. Later, when I was in a bookstore with my wife, I went to the religion section to see if she was still browsing the selections there, and as I turned the corner, one of the books facing out on the shelf was *Pure Act: The Uncommon Life of Robert Lax* by Michael McGregor. My face lit up. I was thrilled and after I read it the first time, I was overjoyed even more. Reading it was pure joy for me. I have underlined many passages and reread them again and again to nourish my soul with gentle joy.

This gentle-man, Robert Lax, called me to take my compassion and prune it so it might welcome others to live their lives more fully. His desire to find more and more of his own gifts, even when he was past eighty years of age, made me realize that the search for God within myself (*imago Dei*) never ceases. There is never a spiritual retirement.

Lax himself shared the impact a person from the East, Brahmachari, had on him: "I feel sure that what held me about him was not so much his ideas...but his personality, and the kind of civilization—the kind of planet—he came from...as though I had always felt there must be that kind of planet somewhere and I was glad to see a representative of it come our way at last."

I feel this way about Menachem Schneerson and Robert Lax. The right biographies early in life can call us to be all that we have been called to be. Later in life, other biographies teach us about wisdom and humility, so we know how to take a step back and deepen our gifts—not just for us to enjoy but so we can share them freely and in a more measured way with others. Might be a nice resolution to read more biographies. Life may be richer because of it.

|||||||||||||||||||||||||||||||||||||||||||||||||||||||||||||||||||||||||||||||||||||||||||||||||||||

16. The Challenge of Empathy

A man whose wife was giving birth to their first child was very anxious. He paced back and forth in the waiting room for what seemed like hours while his wife was in labor. Finally, the nurse came out and announced to him that his wife had just given birth to a healthy child.

In response, he quickly asked, "Is it a boy or a girl?"

"The baby is a girl," she answered.

"Thank heavens!" he immediately replied with an obvious show of great relief on his face. "I am so glad it is a girl instead of a boy because when she grows up and has her first child, she won't have to go through what I have just experienced!"

A priest from Africa shared this story to wake up those listening to his homily on how difficult it can be to see beyond our own little world at times. We often suffer because we are captured by so much in our own little world. The response? Make our world larger by recognizing this: "Everyone you meet is fighting a battle you know nothing about. Be kind. Always."

That message has been attributed to several famous people, but whether it was Plato, Ian Maclaren, Philo, or Robin Williams who said this, the message remains clear: we need to seek the doorway of empathy not only to understand the plight of others but to realize we are not alone and our journey in facing adversity and, in many cases, our crosses are much less than those of others.

In today's "Me Age," this is not easy. It is much simpler to "psychologically and spiritually stay home" rather than face the fear of looking beyond ourselves. Being willing to sit with others and truly be with them also takes energy and patience so healing can take place.

For example, when I began my clinical work and met with sexually abused patients, I was surprised that one of the blocks to healing was that the people around the person who was victimized were often very impatient. They wanted the person to "just get over it."

Whereas the person needed time, a listening ear, and an opportunity to embrace an authentic self that didn't deny or minimize the trauma, but also eventually became free of the psychological and spiritual chains by which they felt bound. In a quote attributed to Shah Rukh Khan, Akshay Dubey, and others, "Healing doesn't mean the damage never existed. It means the damage no longer controls your life."

Healing narcissism and being overly self-involved to the point where empathy is not possible requires attention and patience. Much patience. However we need to attend to it in ourselves, we are to follow Christ in seeking to be there for others. We must lose our (narrow sense of) self if we are to find our true identity. When we are spiritually centered, and because of it not as needy of things, people, and recognition, this becomes more possible. Seeing the obvious narcissism of certain leaders in politics, science, entertainment, sports, and even organized religion is not enough. In observing them and seeking to be empathic to what made them that way as children, we must gently and clearly immediately look in the mirror and ask how we can be freed from ourselves to truly be ourselves. Putting on the new person is not easy and no throwaway line of Scripture. Instead, it is a narrow gate worth walking through.

OPENNESS

17. "Distractions" Are Often the Most Important Events in Life

I have never been good at following directions. When I was a Marine Corps officer, they never let me lead out a platoon for fear we would never find our way back! When I was touring the west of Ireland in a car, finding my way around was challenging to the point of being silly. The first time I passed an area called the Burren, I was amazed at the composition of stone marked by flowers normally seen in such diverse climates as the tropics and more frigid areas. I was also inspired anew when I found myself circling it again. By the fourth time around it, as I tried to find a way out of the area, I became totally frustrated.

Luckily, I saw a man in the distance leaning on the gate to his farm. I thought, Now I can get some directions. As I pulled the car slowly to a stop and got out, he smiled and greeted me warmly. "Lovely day, isn't it?" he said. "The weather is not soft for a change." By this he meant that it had stopped the drizzling rain that had been falling for the past several hours.

I told him about my circling the Burren and needing directions to where I was headed next. He responded by commenting on the Burren, drawing me into conversation about an array of things including myself, and finally sent me off with the directions I needed.

As I drove away, I thought about how nice it was for him to take the time to give me directions. Then, in a flash, I realized that he hadn't simply taken out time from his normal routine; in that encounter and the attention given to it, *he had made me part of his life*.

One of the nicest comments ever made to me was by a student of mine. She said on graduation day that when Bob Wicks stops in the hallway to ask how you are doing, *he means it*.

By being more mindful—attentive to what is going on in the present moment—we can experience life differently than how the culture would have us do today. Society has broken life into tasks and distractions. One Eastern guide admonished that we would all die in the middle of a project and that viewing rushing to our grave as being only practical was quite foolish. We were missing so much. Seeking to be more attentive to the life around us, including not just people but nature as well, and noticing our own feelings in a non-judgmental way is within our reach. We need only practice it more often. Once we do this and see the value, we will do it more often. It will form a positive circle in our life.

18. Failure and "Entertaining Angels"

Recently, a distant memory from Marine Corps Officer Training School came back to me. I was standing by a van with a fellow officer. We were about to enter the van and get teargassed as part of a drill on how to quickly put on your mask to avoid being choked by the fumes. As we stood there and watched each Marine enter the van and then quickly exit it tearing and choking, the other Marine by my side said, take a photo of me when it is my turn. "Really?" I asked. "I want to have a record of this for my children and grandchildren," he replied with a laugh.

While we had a little time before it was our turn, I thought I would tap into his wisdom as a former long-distance runner, because as young lieutenants we often were subjected to dramatic physical endurance tests. The reason was simple: if you expected to lead a platoon of Marines in a forced march, you had better be in better physical shape than they were.

I asked him, "Tell me, Dan, as a former long-distance runner, is there a secret to finishing the race in the best possible time?" My question caught him off guard, so he paused for a moment before answering. After a while he finally said, "Bob, the key is in the pacing. If you run too fast, you will drop before you finish. On the other hand, if you cross the finish line and you feel good, then you know you ran too slow. You didn't give it your all."

"Well, how do you know that your pacing was perfect?" I asked. In response, he smiled and said, "After you cross the finish line, you need to go over to the side of the road and vomit. You have nothing left."

I think something similar can be said in living a life of meaning at times. If you are deeply involved but don't take care of yourself, you won't last the race and will finally give up seeking to be compassionate in creative, constant ways. However, if you never feel like a failure, lost, or that you are not making a difference in this world, then you really are not as involved as you should be.

Recently, I was swept over with feelings that I was truly a failure. I had done some work with people who were very committed and under great stress at the time and I was unsure of my impact. The writing I had also done, into which I had put so much effort, left me with a concern as to whether I was really helping others in what I had written. Finally, a couple of requests I had asked of others when exhausted and in need of help myself were left without a response or with the indication that I had asked too much.

After I experienced this, I was tired, felt rejected, wondered about what good I was really doing, and then recalled two things that made me smile broadly. First, I realized that in feeling this way I was experiencing something that didn't compare with the real difficulties of life that so many others must face. I was guilty of "negative grandiosity." Second, I remembered my chat with the fellow officer by the tear gas van years ago.

If I were to be involved and pace a compassionate life correctly, there would always be times when I would feel like a failure—like the long-distance runner vomiting. It couldn't be avoided and actually needed to be more than endured. Instead, the failure needed to be viewed as a portal to a deeper commitment that included less of my ego, over concern with success or how people reacted, and seen more with a sense of intrigue about my faithfulness in the darkness. Failure was a time to "entertain the angels" of experiencing more deeply the need for God's grace, the realization that we can't do it alone, and that success is not the goal—faithfulness is. I think those certain "angels" only show up when we feel lost, lonely, and a failure. It would be a shame to miss their presence at difficult times in our life, especially because they have such important lessons to teach us that are not available when things are going well.

19. Beauty in Brokenness: Entering "Love Village"

Today, the media often portrays the pains that people experience as the only true reality of life. Simultaneously, anything good that occurs is often glossed over or seen as exceptional. To confront this current falsity, it is important to recognize with a sense of equanimity *both* the unaccountable pain we meet and the goodness within and around us. There is no doubt that much pain in the world is inexplicable and so leads us to wonder why God would allow it to happen. For example, just a few days ago a large vehicle crashed in upstate New York and twenty people were killed, including four sisters and two brothers, who were on their way to a party. How could this have happened? How terrible.

It reminded me of a past event in my life when I was asked to teach a course at Princeton Theological Seminary. One of the students in the course reflected in one of his papers on the result of something terrible that had happened to him with the words, "I didn't think so much sadness could be crammed into a single body."

However, the darkness of suffering need not be the final word; there can be beauty in brokenness. It can even be the first word in new wisdom and light not experienced before.

Recently, I received an email from another former student I taught at a different university who is now a professional clinician and professor herself. One of the comments she wrote in her note reminded me of the Princeton student's words but with an additional, significant spiritual postscript. She shared that in her life she had endured the murder of her son, followed by the death of her husband whose fragile health couldn't survive the trauma of their son's death, and then, following these horrors, the death of a nephew. She said that adjusting to life without the three of them had been and continues to be for her "a grief I never thought I could survive." But then she added the single line that deeply touched me: "Only with God and our love village is it possible."

Later she would tell me, "There is a song that is entitled, 'Beauty in Brokenness.' It is a beautiful gospel song and when I heard it I learned that God's grace provides us beauty even in brokenness." Her husband was very ill for a year before he died, and it gave her and others in the family a chance to have his presence when they most needed it.

As I was in the airport thinking of my impending journey to St. Louis to speak to physician leaders after just traveling back from addressing priests at the Theological College of Catholic University in Washington, D.C., her words echoed in my ears. Up to this point, I had been primarily reflecting on the "lyrics" of my messages—those points that I felt might help the helpers and healers I address to remain resilient. However, I realized once again that just as essential as what I said, was how I sat with them—the "music" or "melody" of my modeling a commitment to their leading a rich and meaningful life might be even more important. They needed to feel I was walking alongside them during their failures, mistakes, anxieties, stresses, and missteps.

When we offer people "space" to be themselves and seek to share our better self, we must never forget God's presence. In addition, we need to seek to become a part of someone's "love village" so that surprisingly good things we could never foresee may happen—not simply to them but to us, too.

The following story demonstrates this well. It is by one of my clinical students who also played the organ and sung at church. I asked her many years ago if I could share it with others in my presentations and book *Riding the Dragon*, and she gave me permission. I am glad she did because it demonstrates the impact we can have on those we haven't even met before. Moreover, the effect may come about in ways that couldn't be expected. When we open ourselves to giving our all, not only in what we are doing but in also offering the interpersonal space for others to face the difficulties in their life, we may become part of a real "love village."

At a funeral, a small somewhat scrawny little boy came upstairs to the music loft to see me after the funeral service. For him to come upstairs alone was a little odd since children usually do not wander around at a funeral. I asked him if he knew where his parents were. He told me in a very matter of fact way, "Well, my mommy is downstairs; she said I could come up to see you. But my daddy is down there now." (He pointed to the casket downstairs.) I immediately crunched down on my teeth, held my breath, and willed myself not to cry, since I was sure this boy had already seen enough tears. But I couldn't help but wonder to myself, "What in the world was his mother thinking to send him up here?!" And I just said, "Oh."

As a counseling student, I am sure there was something much better to say to a seven-year-old boy who had just lost his father, but as it turned out, that one word was enough. It reassured him and gave him enough confidence to tell me, "That song about eagle's wings was my daddy's favorite song and he sung it real loud at church. Now it's *my* favorite song too!"

I couldn't say anything because I had rocks in my throat. He then went over to the balcony and looked down below at the casket sitting in the aisle with the beautiful white lace cover over it. He turned around, looked at me briefly, touched the organ keys very quickly, and ran down the stairs. I tried to say goodbye, but nothing came out.

Several minutes later the widow came upstairs apologizing for her son's intrusion and I reassured her that it was no problem. She then proceeded to tell me that he had not spoken one word or cried or eaten solid food since his dad had died. And she thanked me for my song because it opened him up. She thanked me and, in that moment, I knew it was not solely me who sang but also the melody of the Holy Spirit who reached out and touched that little boy. His name as I learned later was Davie—David Junior—for his dad, and all I will ever know about him is that his favorite song is "On Eagles Wings" by Michael Joncas.

In this brief interaction, my former student unexpectedly became part of that little boy and his mother's life in a crucial way. Then, as she reflected on the few moments of contact she had with them, she experienced entering a circle of grace in her own life. In giving, she had also received. She had entered their "love village" while simultaneously helping them find a road inside this needed spiritual space for them.

That daily possibility and frequent reality, although we might not see it as clearly much of the time, also exists for us if we want it. All it takes are faith and compassion and the "eyes to see" when we take a few quiet moments to reflect not only on life's challenges, but also on its often unwrapped gifts.

20. A Moment for the "Strong Ones"

As an author, sometimes I get so involved in writing even an email that I am oblivious to what is going on around me. However, even when this occurs, fortunately I have an extra sense that allows me to feel when someone is near to me, waiting for an opportunity to say something.

On one of those occasions, as I was almost finishing a delicate message to persons holding the power over others but who seemed to be missing a key element, I looked up from the keyboard and there was a close and talented colleague standing in the doorway. She didn't want to disturb me but obviously wanted to share something that was bothering her.

When I saw her face, I smiled. Though I desperately wanted to complete what I was doing in a manner that was precise, in a gentle voice, I simply said, "What?"

"I see you are busy so if you want," she replied, "I can come back, but I would like to talk to you at some point."

Because she was so resilient and able to handle quite a bit, I was tempted to put her off. However, something in me realized that this would be a mistake. "No," I said. "Now would be good. Come in. Just give me a minute to save what I have been doing. Actually, I could use a break." (I'm not afraid to bend the truth a bit if need be.)

She sat down and related that she was worried about a medical issue. Since she had treated physicians for years and gone the extra mile for them, she felt free enough to ask for professional courtesy to be seen sooner than they initially could schedule her. In response, the receptionist who said she would check to see if this was possible never even called her back as she said she would.

Although she was put off by this, in and of itself, it was not enough to trouble her. However, around the same time, a serious event occurred in her extended family in which she was treated quite poorly. When she stopped for a moment, I asked her, "Well, how did those in your immediate family respond to how you were treated?" She responded in a low voice, "No one even said anything. It was like it didn't happen. I think they were more concerned that I would make a fuss about it."

She went on to tell me that this really didn't surprise her since she was the strong and sane one in her genetic and even extended family but that it hit at a time when she could have used support.

In response, I smiled at her and said, "Well, you are very resilient, flexible, and able to understand the reasons why people behave badly. That is your gift to those around you and the world. Yet you must understand that in being this way, people often forget your needs and don't appreciate that even though you are strong, you could use a moment for support and gentle understanding yourself at times."

She became tearful at that moment, looked up at me, and expressed gratitude that amid all I had on my plate, I had a moment for her. It seemed to make all the difference.

Everyone, including (maybe *especially*) those responsible for the care and support of others, as parents, ministers, therapists, nurses, educators, physicians, and caregivers, need support themselves at times. It is very important that you appreciate this when compassionate souls turn to you for support. If you are "the resilient one" in the family or a system, remember to turn to others who will understand that you need a kind word and occasionally a listening ear, too. Otherwise, you won't make it and that would be a shame.

21. Sensitivity to *Ourselves*

Being a sensitive person isn't just a matter of trying to develop those talents that will help us better attend to others. A sensitive attitude is a seamless garment that begins with an ability to be more sensitive to ourselves as well. Not realizing this can prevent us from being a fully helpful presence to others. In addition, a lack of self-awareness may be dangerous to our own emotional and spiritual well-being. This is particularly evident when we look at a person whose vocation and whole life involves helping others.

For example, at this point, most of my work is with healing and helping professionals such as educators, nurses, physicians, psychologists, social workers, counselors, members of the military, relief workers and organizations, and persons in full-time ministry. When I sit with such caring professionals in distress, at about the tenth session the same feeling always seems to come over me: sadness.

Even though I have heard each of them catalogue their many errors in judgment, past moral lapses, and their major sources of shame ("I *am* someone wrong.") and guilt ("I've *done* something wrong."), I still always have the same feeling of sadness at this point in guiding them. It causes me to reflect: "If only you could see yourself now as I see you. If only you could also see how wonderful and good you are and were able to appreciate, to some degree, the gentle and healing presence you have been to so many people in the world." My hope is that at some point in the mentoring process, or in my presentations to groups in the same position, they will achieve this recognition.

Obviously, this failure to appreciate the goodness of God in themselves while simultaneously seeing it in others is not limited to the talented and caring persons with whom I interact. I think the same can be said of all of us who wish to be sensitive and live a life that is both centered and meaningful. If we want to piece the darkness of callousness within and around us to embrace the peace that is always present and possible, we must be willing to appreciate our own signature strengths and efforts as well as welcome a loving God in new refreshing ways. Otherwise, we are not going to make it as compassionate people. It's as simple as that.

22. A Great Challenge in the Spiritual Life

When we look at any Sacred Scripture, whether it is the New Testament, the Hebrew Scriptures, Vedanta, the Koran, or the Upanishads, we will see the challenge put before us to give, to love. In the New Testament we see this especially in the controversial epistle of James. Essentially, the message is, "Put up or shut up!" It echoes the Chinese proverb, "Talk doesn't cook rice."

But as essential as the challenge is to be loving to others in how we live, I don't believe it is the greatest challenge in the spiritual life.

I think the truly most demanding challenge is not to give love but to *receive* love. Embracing this reality not only has great import for the person who embraces this challenge but also for those around them who are in a position to be recipients of their compassion and care.

We see this in the words of Pope John XXIII who reminded us that whoever has a heart full of love always has something to share. It is also multicultural so we will see it in the proverbs of many different people. For example, the Ibo of Nigeria have a saying: It is the heart that gives; the fingers just let go.

Without the ability to receive the love that is around us, our giving can become too compulsive, conditional, and tentative. Without having a deep sense of being loved, we are not really able to give with a sense of *mitzvah*—giving and expecting nothing in return. Rather, we share with a sense of expectancy. If people don't show gratitude or follow our suggestions (which by the way, they rarely do!), rather than humbly understanding why this may happen, we can feel let down, hurt, depressed, angry, or "used." The dangers of this seem evident today in persons at the head of government, sometimes surprisingly in those providing social services, and even at times in the case of religious leaders. (Recently, I heard a newspaper reporter covering a national religious event remark about a bishop after he made a sarcastic comment, "He is not very humble, is he?")

But if we are continually open to receiving love, we don't worry as much about people's reactions. We simply give and leave it at that. The process is rewarding in itself.

Whereas the problem is that if we have not taken steps to unlearn our assumptions, expectations, and demands of others, and can't let go of our "neediness" for positive responses from them, we cannot learn simple new ways to receive the love that is already around us. Therefore, our true, loving attitude won't last very long.

We will not feel replenished, and we will become even more inclined to rely on those whom we reach out to for our restoration—at *best*, a very precarious situation! Being able to appreciate new ways of experiencing love (a real relearning process) is essential for those wishing to live a compassionate, generative life.

Such a life carries with it a deep sense of meaning, purpose, peace, and perspective *if* we are not too stubborn in our designation of what love is for us. For example, when I have given positive feedback at times to some people, you can see in their eyes what they're thinking: "Oh, he is a spiritual mentor and psychologist and they say nice things like that." It is like the old joke: "Who would want to join a club that would accept me?"

Once again, to emphasize a habit I spoke of earlier, we tend to hear praise in a whisper and negative things as thunder and never question why this is the case so we can correct for it.

The challenge that Sacred Scripture gives us to love others is certainly matched by our challenge to see where we are not finding the love that is already there in *our* life.

This keystone to both psychological and spiritual self-esteem is also important because it allows us to be more honest in the way we view ourselves and others. Those of us who feel loved are not only able to see, rejoice, and freely share the many gifts we have been given while expecting and needing little in return, we are also able to look at our faults and shortcomings without also condemning ourselves in the process. We can see everything in others with a sense of inquisitiveness because we are using the same process in our own self-discovery process. When this happens, we can feel the wonder of life even when surrounded by difficult situations and people. That is a pretty good gift to ourselves, don't you think? And that gift is only a small part of the love that God is giving us if we are willing to see it as that and not ignore or dismiss such divine presents.

In John 15, we hear the words from Jesus, "You are my friend." We need to take steps to see how we are turning our back on such statements—not as a journey in narcissism and denial but to the contrary: so we can face our own lacks with a sense of honesty, without being unnerved by our faults, and so we can give to others out of our feeling abundant love rather than a need to be thanked, followed, or admired.

23. An Unrecognized Teacher in Our Midst

Once, when teaching a graduate course on the integration of psychology and classic spirituality, I noticed a fascinating dynamic between two of the students. One was a Buddhist and the other was an Evangelical Christian. The Buddhist modeled a sense of serenity, while the Evangelical Christian was passionate and would sometimes be quite expressive. I noticed when she would be so outgoing with her feelings and opinions, it would be quite disturbing for the Buddhist, who was sitting right in front of me. In response, he would make facial expressions that only I could see. I kept my observations of his reactions to myself.

Then one day the student who was quite effusive became so excited about something that she ended up throwing an object at the board just missing me. Of course, she was mortified and later shared with me that she recognized her need to look at her behavior, which I reinforced because I knew that, with some mentoring, her deep passion could find greater focus and produce better results for her and those with whom she interacted.

After this outburst on her part, however, the young Buddhist counseling student in front of me could not contain his disdain for her behavior. I felt it was time to "take advantage" of his reaction to help him to search further within himself, and I asked him at the end of class if he would remain.

When everyone had left, I said to him, "You noticed the behavior of the student who threw something at the board." He responded quite vehemently that he did and that the psychological dike broke open as he laid out his negative feelings toward her. Once he was done, in a low voice I said to him, "She is your spiritual guide." In response, you could see the incredulous look on his face before he commented, "I'll have to think about that." To which I said, "I didn't ask you to think about it. She is your spiritual director." Then I walked out, leaving him to reflect on what I had said so firmly.

My point to this very psychologically and spiritually mature student was that he was ready to see that anything and anyone who was able to elicit that much negative emotion was actually a "teacher" to him about what he found most upsetting, fearful, anxiety-provoking, or a cause for anger rather than sorrow. When we can listen to those whom we find we don't like in a way that calls us deeper to examine our own virtues, much can be learned about ourselves, and little is left for projection of blame onto others. Moreover, as the Dalai Lama once noted, "A person who practices compassion and forgiveness has greater inner strength, whereas aggression is usually a sign of weakness." If only this lesson could be learned by us and today's politicians, it would be a more peaceful world guided forth by more humble leaders.

As I have now passed the age of seventy, I had to smile when I read the following words of Polish-born rabbi, theologian, and philosopher Abraham Joshua Heschel: "When I was young, I used to admire intelligent people; as I grow older, I admire kind people." To this I would only add that at this stage of my life I also feel the need to be kinder, and I wish I had done better in the past. People are suffering in so many ways we don't know about, so a little spontaneous kindness can be a salve for the wounds they recognize, as well as the unconscious ones they are not able to see. It is certainly worth the effort, even when we don't see the results we had hoped for or receive gratitude for our efforts.

‖‖‖

24. Honor Your Pain and Embrace Your Joy: A Delicate Balance Is Needed, Especially for Compassionate Souls

Children's words and facial expressions often stay with me. In my many different roles as parent, grandparent, therapist, mentor of caregivers, and as an author, they seem to burn into my memory in positive and challenging ways.

For example, years later I still remember seeing a photo of my oldest granddaughter opening a Christmas gift of a toy "doctor's kit." Her facial expression was priceless! It was filled with surprise and pure joy. For me it symbolized not only her inner spirit but the joy all of us have when we spontaneously receive something hoped for but totally unexpected.

On the other side of the equation, challenging comments and images also stay with me. After returning from working with care-givers from Aleppo, Syria, who were brought to Beirut, Lebanon, so I might guide them in ways to remain resilient, I received an email from a Marist Brother. In the message he shared the challenges they had returned to after I left and the voice of a young Syrian girl who asked him, "Why am I losing the best years of my life? Why am I not like the rest of the girls in the world? Why do I not have the right to live fully my youth? Is this God's will? Why does he not answer our prayers and pleas? In spite of our trust in him, we do not see the end of this tunnel."

In response, the Marist Brother reflected, "What answer can I give her and to many other young persons? I listen to them. I support them. I try to seek to stutter words of trust and of faith. This is not always easy. Our young people [in Syria] live anguished. They seek to leave, to get out of this hell without precedence. The parents come to ask for advice. What can we say?"

Like this Brother, when I recently heard of a little girl dying of dehydration just inside the U.S. border, I can neither turn my back nor offer solutions. The same can be said of us, when in our families we are confronted by the sudden death of a loved one, a diagnosis of a chronic illness that a young person must carry with her all her life, serious financial stress, marital pressures, drug abuse, and any of the other pressures, anxieties, and uncertainties life presents fami-lies today. When they occur, we must face them directly. Hiding from them by offering spiritual platitudes, trying to forget or minimize them, or psychologically avoiding any pain in life just doesn't work.

What does help in facing our own and others pain though, is to take conscious steps to prevent ourselves and others from simulta-neously missing the joys that happen to come our way. I have seen caregivers experiencing what we call "traumatic countertransference" do exactly that when they felt too guilty to enjoy their own lives while others are suffering. The reality though is that when a helper, parent, or friend does this because of others' pain, they will eventually lose their own resilience and be of little use to those who depend on them for support during the darkness they are experiencing.

Yes, we must honor our pain and that of others by facing it, doing what we can, and not playing down how it is impacting us. Running away by minimizing suffering or avoiding facing what we must by calling it "fake news" is not helpful. Yet simultaneously not *fully taking in the joys of life*, when they present themselves to us, is also not only foolish—it is wrong! After all, isn't one of the reasons some of Jesus's leading disciples were able to travel the difficult road into Jerusalem to face the challenges they were called to meet because they didn't close their eyes to the joy of the transfiguration when they were privileged to experience and internalize it?

By all means, fully enjoy the presents of life. They are the gifts of people and things we have been fortunate to receive. Not only will embracing them allow your facial expression to be more like my granddaughter's when she opened her toy doctor's kit, it will also provide the strength needed to help others, as well as yourself, to deal with life's challenges, big and small, that all of us must face at different times.

FREEDOM

25. "You Can, Too!"

On March 23, 2017, President Bill Clinton traveled to Derry, Northern Ireland, to deliver the eulogy for Martin McGuinness at St. Columba's Church. During his presentation, he shared a telephone conversation he had with Nelson Mandela after he had become president of South Africa.

Mandela had called and said that he was getting so much criticism. Clinton asked him if it was from the Afrikaners. Mandela told him, "No. No. It was from my own people. They think I've sold them out." Clinton then asked him, "Well, what did you tell them?" In reply, Mandela told Clinton that he responded to them by saying, "Yes, and I spent 27 years in jail, they took the best years of my life away, I didn't see my children grow up, it ruined my marriage, and a lot of my friends were killed. And, if I can get over it, *you* can too! We've got to build a future."

To a great degree, the quality of our future actions and life depends on what we can face, learn, and let go of from our past. The human person has only so much energy and inner psychological space. If our lives become chained to past unfinished business, then we will not have the ability to think, plan, and live in the present and meet the future with a sense of freedom.

Once, a patient of mine shared something that he was angry about. When I asked him what about it made him angry, rather than responding to the question, he leaned forward in his chair and screamed, "Well, wouldn't *you* be angry?" In response, I told him that things hit different people in different ways. Now he also seemed to be annoyed with me for not understanding his predicament, and we explored what that was about as well.

Toward the end of the session, after we had examined the genesis of his anger in the situation, and now with me, we then had a chance to switch gears to the theme of the advantage of being able to get over something by working it through. In doing so, I gave him the image of grasping a hot poker.

I noted that if you were unfortunate to grab a hot poker, screaming in pain would be a natural and understandable immediate response. From the beginning of time, screaming has been a survival instinct. A scream alerts us and others that there is a danger present. However, continuing to hold onto the hot poker and screaming is not such a good idea. When we don't get over what has been done to us, or something unpleasant we have done, that is just what we are doing. We are letting someone else's, or our own wrongdoing, disempower us.

Letting go doesn't mean forgetting or diminishing what has

happened. Nor does it deny that it hurt us or someone else. Instead, it is a process of allowing things to take their proper perspective in the present so we don't compound the difficulty by wasting our energy tying ourselves to what has been done to us or has happened that we regret or don't like. If Nelson Mandela can get over it to build the future of his nation, we can get over it to build the future of our lives. But, of course, this is not easy and takes a great deal of commitment, faith, perseverance, and sometimes a great, great deal of patience. It cannot and should not be rushed. (Family, friends, and even therapists sometimes inadvertently do this with victims of abuse.)

The philosopher Jean-Paul Sartre once said, that living well is both difficult and possible. People don't like to hear that today, so they separate the quote. Some would rather have us believe it is easy or magical to live a good life. It is not. Others would have us feel it is impossible. It is not. The more challenging but rewarding stance is to recognize, as Sartre suggests, that living life fully is both difficult and possible. When we embrace this reality, like Mandela, we can take an amazing journey going forward that benefits not just us but those around us as well.

––

26. Failure and Forgiveness of *Yourself*

In "resiliency psychology and spirituality," my specialty for the past thirty years, one of the more recent areas of discussion and emphasis is referred to as "self-compassion." This may sound to some like narcissism or inordinate self-interest. However, a real understanding of self-compassion shows us that this is far from an accurate understanding of it. Instead, healthy self-compassion has a proportionate impact on our ability to walk with others in their darkness. This is so because one of the greatest gifts we can share with others is a sense of our own peace and inner strength, but we can't share what we don't have!

An essential cornerstone of such appropriate self-compassion is the ability to forgive yourself when you fail. Involved, spiritually committed persons fail a great deal. We probably don't like to talk about it, but it's true. As a group, we fail as much if not *more* than any other community concerned with helping others in need. This should not be surprising since with greater commitment there is a greater "opportunity" to miss at least some of the numerous goals we set for ourselves in life.

Yet, despite the fact that as persons of faith we court failure as a natural part of our idealism, many of us still punish ourselves mentally when we feel we have missed the mark, even if it was an almost impossible one. One of the most powerful ways of dealing with such a tendency is to embrace a proper sense of forgiveness about what we have failed to do or accomplish in our work with others or in facing our own shortcomings or sins.

To accomplish this, we must first recognize and avoid false forms of forgiveness. "Pseudo-forgiveness" often parades itself as a form of true self-awareness. By its "fruits," however, it is possible to discern in ourselves and others whether the sense of forgiveness is properly oriented. There are surely numerous forms of pseudo-forgiveness. The one that particularly concerns us here is the one that forgets our humanity, inordinately focuses on the shame of our failures, and leads to an unproductive confession based only on ventilation of our shortcomings or sins.

Pseudo-forgiveness of self begins when in trying to be compassionate we forget that we can and *will* eventually fail. We forget that in trying to reach out to family, friends, coworkers, and even those in need whom we do not know well, our own limits and needs must sometimes get in the way. When I was lecturing a group of surgical residents on resilience, self-care, and healthy perspective, I cautioned them with the reality that during their tenure as surgeons, they would probably kill some people—not necessarily because of malpractice but because of "*mis*-practice." No one can operate on an "A" level 100 percent of the time, no matter what their role. Parents do get tired and yell at their children even when they recognize (possibly later) that this was not the best thing to do. Others are sometimes short-tempered or condescending to the poor or chronically ill in their midst when they are not fully rested, have eliminated the space for personal "alone-time" (periods of silence and solitude or being reflective even when in a group), or don't have enough balance in their schedule. At such times, it is easy to forget that we are not perfect—only God is—and that with the right outlook we can learn from our failures rather than see them simply as proof that we shouldn't, or *can't*, be a compassionate presence to others in need.

When we as people trying to be spiritually faithful lose our perspective regarding failure, we ignore the need for self-acceptance as a prelude to personal growth. In such cases, instead of forgiveness leading to an openness that will in turn translate into greater self-understanding, it leads to self-punishment or condemning others for their needs and situation. In such a case as this, we believe that we are seeking forgiveness by crucifying ourselves for our weakness. As we do this, the energy formerly reserved for knowledge gets destructively channeled off into changing the process of self-understanding into one of self-condemnation. Nothing positive is accomplished when this happens.

Ironically, this hurtful process of supposedly honest repentance *prevents* rather than enhances change and growth. The most obvious reason for this is that we are less apt to look at our behavior objectively if we are embarrassed or pained by reflection on it. Therefore, behavior that we wince at eventually turns into behavior that we wink at. If it causes us too much discomfort to look at something, psychologically we will avoid it through repression, suppression, denial, rationalization, and by general distortion of it.

So, how can we mine the fruits of personal failure when it occurs? First, I think our *attitude* is key. It will determine if we can weather the storms of failure and a sense of loss when our goals are not achieved. In her memoir, *Dakota*, author Kathleen Norris wrote that she was called to reflect on this when she had come across a handwritten note by her grandmother inserted in an old family Bible. On it was written, "Keep me friendly to myself; keep me gentle in disappointment."

The second element is *clarity*. While we need to recognize the need to be kind so that we don't cause narcissistic injury (hurt ourselves to the core of our personality), we also need to seek details about our failures, losses, and disappointments. If we are only gentle, we won't grow. If we only focus on our failures in a nonforgiving way, we will stunt our own growth. We need a balance of clarity and kindness in facing failure and forgiving ourselves for not being the person we wish to be in all situations.

The final element on the way to healthy self-forgiveness is to recognize that failure can teach us in much more powerful ways than success ever can. If we have the right balance of clarity and kindness, we will

- Experience increased motivation and determination to face what we encounter as "darkness" or failure in ourselves.
- Gain greater insight into who we are as persons because we will uncover our gifts, areas of vulnerability, and defenses.
- Have less dependence on the recognition and approval of others.
- Be in a better position to pick up more quickly the emotional cues that we are going to do something we will regret so we can stop ourselves.
- Set the stage for the development of new skills and styles of interacting with others, especially in tough or chronically draining situations.
- Appreciate, like St. Paul, that we must never shy away from seeing our failings or shortcomings clearly. Also like Paul, however, we must ensure that in the same breath we must always also speak of God's grace so we don't fall into the trap of the "savior complex" and think we must never fail or have problems forgiving ourselves.
- Know we can't ride the waves of life's stresses alone and expect we can always achieve our goals and gain the perspective on our own, to know how and when to forgive ourselves. As Reinhold Niebuhr, American ethicist, theologian, and commentator, aptly notes, "Nothing we do, however virtuous, can be accomplished alone."
- Finally, forgiveness of self also involves patience with oneself so we can recognize that living a compassionate

life involves tolerating discouragement and having
the fortitude to continue in spite of the absence of
immediate results. As Thomas Merton once said to a
senior Trappist colleague who felt he was losing both
his commitment and faith, "Brother, courage comes
and goes...hold on for the next supply!"

Essentially, when we truly understand the need for forgiveness
of self when we fail, as we surely will at times, we will position ourselves to have a greater sense of inner peace that is independent of
external success, comfort, and security. When we have such an attitude, think of what a gift that would be not only to ourselves but also
to those we co-journey with as friend, family member, coworker or
in a possibly professional role as helper or healer. Self-forgiveness is
not a nicety. It is a necessity in today's anxious world.

||||||||||||||||||||||||||||||||||||||||||||||||||||||||||||||||||||||||||||||||||||||||||

27. Don't Give Away Your Joy

One of the great blessings in my life is that I have had the
opportunity to lecture in Ireland several times on resilience, self-
care, and maintaining a healthy perspective. On one of those visits, I
had a hilarious encounter with the person hosting me. Upon landing
at the airport, she greeted me with the following words shared a bit
breathlessly with a light brogue, "My gosh, you must be exhausted!"
To which I responded, "No I feel great. I took a week off before I had
to fly here and we flew Aer Lingus, so it felt like we were having a
party on board."

Not to be dissuaded, she added, "But you will be jumping in
here and killing yourself, now." To which I then added, "I love it here
in Ireland. Your scenery is great, but it is the people here that are the
best. Even your road signs. They are basically just hints. I just *love* it!"

"But after lecturing here," she continued, "you will be going back
and working in America." "No," I said. "I will take another week off
before I have to start again." To which she said, "Oh, you can't kid me.
You keep a tough schedule." I held my ground and responded by saying, "Actually, I will be teaching then for three weeks up in Vermont

at St. Michael's College. It is so much fun, I don't know why they even pay me."

"Ah, sure, it still is taxing." To which I replied with a smile, "Then, after teaching at St. Mike's I will be taking a long weekend off at Martha's Vineyard." At this point, totally frustrated at my not wanting to be tagged a martyr, she stopped, blinked, and said, "My God, you take a lot of time off, don't you?"

All of us have had friends, family, coworkers, and passing acquaintances who meant well in what they have said to us but were, in fact, producing the opposite effect. With some people you can ventilate and feel better. With others as soon as you say something about having a bit of a hard time, they jump in and seem to make it worse rather than better.

One of the ways to prevent this from happening is to renew our sense of gratitude each day. Brother David Steindl-Rast once pointed out that we often leave the house each day with a mental list, and on that list is what we will be grateful for. He suggests that we throw this preconceived list away so we can be open to seeing new places in our life in which we are being blessed.

For those in the helping and healing professions, as well as those responsible for family members and others, this can be difficult at times. Zen Master Thich Nhat Hanh once noted that during the middle of the Vietnam War they were so busy concentrating on the suffering that they sometimes forgot to take in the wondrous scents of the country. He said that particularly in the rural areas, if they were attentive, they could be buoyed by the smell of mint, coriander, sage, and thyme. I was lecturing in Hanoi to international caregivers a couple of years ago. During a day off amid the work, as I was in a canoe traveling up one of the rivers in the countryside, I could experience these very fragrances.

Gratitude allows those of us who have been given so much and are called to be compassionate with what we have and who we are, to experience even more to be grateful for in different ways. One of the most effective approaches to accomplish this is through friends who encourage and help us to realize that while our tasks may be difficult, there are always *lights in the darkness that will never go out if only we have the eyes to see.* This is important, not just for us, but for those who rely on our joy and presence during difficult dark times.

28. "Sleep Faster—We Need the Pillows!": Stress, Self-Care, Resilience, and Maintaining a Healthy Perspective

The above Yiddish proverb certainly describes what many of us feel today. The unrealistic expectations and raw emotions of others in need confront not only helping and healing professionals but touch almost all of us who wish to be compassionate. Still, as I travel and speak on resilience, self-care, and maintaining a healthy perspective to professionals and the general public, two things strike me again and again.

First, the overwhelming needs of others arise in ways and at times that often surprise us. When I was at Dover Air Force Base, I heard that one of the volunteers working with families of the fallen was confronted by a little boy whose father in the military had lost his life in the Middle East. The little boy looked up at the volunteer as the death finally was becoming more of a reality to him and asked, "Who will play ball with me now?"

When speaking at the 92nd Street Y on my book *Perspective*, a woman of about 50 years of age came up to me after my talk and said, "I was just diagnosed with Stage 4 cancer, I see my surgeon this week, and am very afraid of what I will hear. Can you help me with how I feel?" Two weeks later, when I was at Notre Dame speaking to healthcare executives, one of the persons attending my presentations on maintaining a healthy perspective said to me, "You and your book have come at just the right time for me. Two months ago, my twenty-six-year-old son suddenly died."

The pressing needs and unanswerable questions of others surround all of us in different ways today. Yet there is another thing that strikes me as being worth noting: that the listening space we offer others, in and of itself, is a major help. A woman who had suffered a major sexual trauma when she was little and was seeing me as an adult showed this to me in a simple, yet powerful, way. I asked her at the end of her therapy with me, "How did you get to this point? You weren't this way when you first came in to see me." In asking this, I knew that once she left therapy, she would enter darkness again at times since it comes and goes for all of us who care. I hoped my question would provoke her bringing to mind an array of techniques that she could use to face such future difficult times more gently and effectively. Yet she surprised me when she replied, "Oh, it was simple. The first time I came in to see you I simply watched how you sat with me and then I began sitting with myself in the same way." She had borrowed and learned from the respectful space she received from me.

The problem is that we can't share what we don't have. Unless we have an inner sense of peace, a healthy perspective, and become freer from our own sometimes exaggerated self-involvement, how can we offer space to others? I have spent my whole professional life developing a list of suggestions with this question in mind. I enjoy presenting them in person as well as in my writings, especially my three books *Night Call*, *Riding the Dragon*, and *Bounce*. But the key list of some of what I think we need to remember can save a reading of these works or attending one of my presentations. They include the following:

1. **Have a balanced circle of friends** who challenge, humor, and support you. All too often, we settle for having friends and family who can't do this because they are unable to for some reason. A good interpersonal network can make all the difference.

2. **Be faithful to being compassionate** because only being concerned about yourself will make you unhappy. When you are overly self-involved, your life will become too small. It is like putting a spoon of salt in a small glass; you will taste the bitterness of life. Whereas, when you reach out to others, it is like putting a spoon of salt in a lake. The bitterness

dissolves amid a wider appreciation of others' gifts and needs.

3. **Keep healthy self-compassion sitting alongside compassion for others**, so that instead of burning out, you can enjoy keeping the flame lit for both yourself and others. Developing your own "self-care protocol or program" helps in this regard. It should be both ambitious and realistic.

4. **Lean back** when you feel the negative behavior, attitude, or emotions of others are seeking to pull you in. You don't want to be callous, but the opposite of detachment is not caring involvement, it is seduction by others' sad or angry behavior, as well as their unrealistic expectations. They may not intentionally mean to behave this way, but if I drop a rock on your head on purpose or by mistake, you still get a bump. Learn to "move your head" by leaning back from the emotions of others.

There is a lot more, of course, but I try to keep the above in mind—especially when dealing with difficult situations and people—so I thought I would share them. It helps me to learn about my own large ego, have better insight into what is causing others to inflict pain on themselves, and be better able to persevere with those who have been victimized or are having difficulty opening themselves up to other views of life. But more importantly, it helps me to benefit as I continue my work with educators, physicians and nurses, psychologists, psychiatrists, counselors, social workers, members of the military, and persons in full-time ministry. Because in reaching out to them with the right space within me, I get to see something wonderful again and again: good people doing great things. It really makes my day and inspires me to not just see the darkness but also all the good that is going on in this world. What a blessing they are to me and my continual need to maintain a healthy perspective.

29. Visiting Maspeth: Lessons on Impermanence and How They Can Change the Way We Live

On a trip from Pennsylvania with my wife for a wedding anniversary on Long Island, we were passing through the borough of Queens in New York City. Since we would be passing through Maspeth, the city where I was born and raised, I suggested we stop for a cup of coffee and then walk around a bit. We were ahead of schedule and I thought it would be fun to walk past my old house and see how the neighborhood had changed.

My house was completely redone, which wasn't a total surprise because it was over a hundred years old when we lived in it. I used to tease that if the termites ever stopped holding hands, the place would collapse. What was disappointing to me though was that they had paved over the little grass covered yard. They had made it into a mini parking lot for their car. As I stood there, taking in what was different, I wondered to myself how many other changes had taken place in the neighborhood as well.

We then walked down to the end of the street because I wanted to see a house where I had spent a great deal of time at as a teenager. A friend of mine, who was in my wedding party, had lived upstairs, and his cousin, who was my first girlfriend, lived downstairs. I loved their parents and had great fun in the many gatherings we had there while I was in high school.

Their house had even fared less well than mine. It looked worn and the yard a bit overgrown. In walking through the neighborhood, I noticed that while there were still nice tree-lined streets, there were blocks that looked almost shabby. I was surprised that many neighborhood stores had also changed to accommodate the new likes and desires of the many new people that had moved into the area.

Upon returning home after my nostalgia tour, I decided to do a search on the Web for both my friend and his cousin. I didn't expect to find too much on my male friend. Years ago, I did a search and found only bits and pieces that had to do with his time as a city police officer. When I searched for his cousin, I didn't turn up anything. However, since the neighborhood had stirred up thoughts of my youth, I felt I had nothing to lose.

In looking up my friend Billy, I expected to see his smiling face in uniform as a young police officer. Instead, my heart dropped when I saw a listing sponsored by a funeral home: he had died a year ago. Once into the site, I found his obituary and a nice photo taken of him and his wife at some reception. Next, I looked up his cousin, Joanne, expecting to find nothing. But she was also listed in *another* obituary. She had died a year ago as well—two weeks before her cousin Billy. On the funeral parlor's site, there were an array of photos dating from when I last had seen her fifty years ago, through the aging process, until the final photo of her posted as a frail person who was obviously quite ill.

What surprised me more than their death was my profound reaction to my discovery that they were gone. The three of us had moved through life on very different paths. We had very, very little in common. I also hadn't seen either of them in over half a century. In Billy's case, I had at least spoken to him over the telephone when he made the effort to track down and call me about five years earlier. I then had sent him some of the books that I had written, and we spoke one more time over the telephone. Even in this conversation, which centered on our youth, and on his briefing me a bit about the people we both knew years ago, I could tell that we would soon run out of things to speak about. We were just in different places in life. Other than sending him a book at a later date and thinking about surprising him with my book *Night Call*, since that book meant so much to me, we never spoke again. In the case of Joanne, I hadn't seen or been in contact with her for over 50 years. There never seemed any need and I didn't even consider it. She and her husband, who had also been a friend of mine, were off the radar.

Yet, when I heard they had died, two thoughts immediately struck me. The first was that I would have liked to have said goodbye to them both. I felt cheated of closure. The second was that I sensed strongly that with their deaths my teenage and young adult years had been closed for good. I felt the slamming of a spiritual and psychological steel door, which would be permanently locked. The experiences of my early life felt like they were gone forever or that only fragments remained.

As part of processing the whole experience to better understand what I was going through, I mentioned it to several people. Everyone was kind, supportive, and understanding, but somehow I felt that I couldn't capture for them the depth and sadness of the encounter and its aftermath. Yet something important was here for me to fathom at a deeper level than might have been possible before, so I continued to meditate about it.

One of the important lessons that arose was certainly tied to the issue of "impermanence." We tend to deny or avoid our mortality through activity and a busy lifestyle that includes yet one more thing to do. Our behavior often demonstrates that we believe it is "practical" to run toward our grave. Enjoying silence and solitude takes a back seat in our schedule unless we have run out of everything else to do on our list.

A wonderful encounter that I had when I was teaching at Loyola University Maryland was when I was interacting with a younger colleague as her mentor. I still remember one of the most emotional encounters. I was typing a manuscript and she poked her head in the door. I looked up and asked, "What?" She replied, "Do you have a minute?" I could see from her face that she was going through something and that this would take more than a minute. I was about to ask if we could schedule a time to meet since I was in the middle of the project I was working on when she added, "They're messing with me." She had been in the U.S. navy earlier in her career, so she used a more colorful word than *messing*. I responded with a smile on my face, "Well, we can't have that, can we?"

She came in and discussed how she had felt let down by someone whom she thought "had her back" and why the assessment of her work over the past year was unfair. After listening to both the content of what she was saying and noting her emotions, I commiserated and then helped her structure a response. I said I would also send an email to the persons she was referring to. Before we departed, she said to me, "Next to my husband and my father, I count on you most." I was deeply touched by her comment and said so.

We then briefly chatted about the different pieces of her life:

being involved in the parish, a wife and mother of five girls, a psychologist, an author, professor, and only forty years of age. When we had finished, I said to her, you are the whole package. Yet there is one area I would like you to think about. She stopped and I could tell she was intrigued by what I would say. I then added, "You need some quiet time in your life. Some moments of silence and solitude where you can meet yourself and God in ways that everything else will benefit." She responded by saying what so many of us say, "I realize it is important. If only I could make the time." Then she got up and went back to work.

Several months later, her husband left a message for me to call him. He had never done this, so I was surprised and quickly returned his call. He responded by telling me that his wife, my younger colleague and friend, had taken four of their five daughters to the swimming club. After they were there for a while, it started to rain. She gathered them up to go home, and they got into the van and were stopped for a light on Connecticut Avenue in Washington, D.C., when a large limb from an enormous tree fell onto the van, crushing her and one of her children: they were both dead. A woman who was touted on the front page of *The Washington Post* as a "Super Mom" and one of her children who was filled with an infectious sense of energy were suddenly gone.

As I mentioned earlier, a more recent incident occurred when I was asked to speak on resilience at Dover Air Force Base in Delaware. The goal was to speak to members of the unit responsible for returning fallen military and for the support of their families. As I stood in the beautiful house they had reserved for the families to stay so they could attend the ceremonies honoring their dead relative, I heard about the reaction of one of the children of a fallen serviceman. As he stood there in the hallway of the house trying to take in the fact that his father was gone, he suddenly blurted out to one of the volunteers, "Who will play ball with me now?" A young person was confronted with the reality of impermanence and death early on in his own life. Upon hearing this, a sudden sadness came over me, and I thought, "I wonder whether as time goes on this darkness will be a reminder for him that life, *his* life, is very precious, and, as for us all, quite brief.

Michel de Montaigne in his *Selected Essays* shared a story of a group of people in Africa who put a skull on the table during big celebrations. This was not done to depress and curb the merriment of those present. To the contrary, it was to remind them to value their celebrations because life is so short.

It is with this deep sense of the reality that we and all those around us will not be here forever that helps us see life differently. It is easier to keep things in perspective, remember to value the truly important things, and not to get carried away by what is unimportant—no matter what the world might tell us—that is a gift. In light of this, encountering our own hometowns and deaths of those whom we know are not simply doorways to the darkness of loss. They can also be the beginning of seeing the infinite pathway in new, more pressing, and enlightening ways. For this to happen, however, we can't turn our back on death, sadness, loss, or the seemingly "little" events and reactions of each day. Instead, we need to involve ourselves and reflect on our reactions so that the "field notes" that we prepare mentally or in writing can trace new learnings.

30. Unnecessary Personal Darkness

The darkness we experience in life often tells just as much about us as it does about what we feel is its cause. In some cases, what it does reveal is that the darkness we encounter is unnecessary if we are willing to be more honest from the start in our sensitivity to ourselves.

Some people always seem to be making trouble for themselves. With such moody individuals it seems as though every third Tuesday marks the arrival of yet another "dark night of the soul." (In such cases, the real darkness is usually experienced by those who have to interact with such personality types!). However, in less extreme cases—which hopefully is the category in which you and I fit—there is also a need to recognize that many of our problems are of our own making. This will keep us from trivializing the significant experience that John of the Cross and others have referred to as "darkness" or the psychological and physical symptoms of "clinical depression."

Much of what we face that we find dark and difficult, unfortunately, is partly of our own doing in this world. Yoda, the wisdom figure or "Jedi Master," made this point in the movie *The Empire Strikes Back* from the original *Star Wars* trilogy that was so popular in the 1980s. In this movie, Yoda urged Luke Skywalker, the young man who was his disciple, to enter a cave that seemed to emanate danger and fear. When young Luke asked Master Yoda, "What's in there?" his simple response was, "Only what you take with you."

The same can be said of us as we enter "the cave of the tiger" in prayer and reflection. Many things from a myriad of sources will tear at us. But chief among them are our interior demons. For many of us, they include some of the following:

- Lack of self-awareness, self-acceptance, and self-love
- Dishonesty
- Intolerance of others
- Unfinished business with family and friends
- Consciously suppressed and unconsciously repressed negative feelings
- Poorly developed ethics, beliefs, and values
- Inordinate attachments or addictions
- Hidden past or unintegrated embarrassments
- Resistance to intimacy
- Failure to take care of yourself physically
- Lack of honesty and openness in prayer and self-reflection
- Lack of meaning in life
- Ungrieved losses
- Greed
- Unreasonable expectations of self and others
- A sense of entitlement
- Unresolved anger
- Unwillingness to risk and an inordinate need for security
- Inability to experience quiet in your life
- Unhealthy self-involvement or, at the other extreme, lack of a healthy self-interest

- Failure to set priorities in life
- Irresponsibility
- Being overly perfectionistic and inordinately self-critical
- Unwillingness to accept love except in ways one has predetermined as meaningful ("If _____ doesn't love me, then the warmth and acceptance in my life isn't important.")
- Fear of responsibility and a tendency to project blame
- Resistance to change

The darkness of a true encounter with self can be like a "psychological or spiritual mirror" that crisply reflects those partially hidden and disguised parts of our personality that keep us chained to a sense of life that isn't open or mature enough. It reflects our own rigid defenses, personal immaturities, unresolved repressed issues, hidden motivations, tenacious defenses, erroneous (yet comfortable) self-definitions, and our chameleon-like behaviors. Essentially, it confronts us with the darkness of our unintegrated self.

Yet, although such information may initially put us off, if we can look at it with a sense of intrigue, while remembering the unconditional love of God and good friends and family, it can set us free. Who wouldn't want to be freer to live and enjoy a meaningful life?

⁣⁣⁣

31. Convenient Giving or True Generosity

Several years ago, the wife of a friend of mine died. Not long after it, he gave away some of her possessions to an in-house aide who came in to help several times a week. I could tell by the way he shared the story that he was proud of what he had done. He expected that she would be very grateful for what he perceived as his great generosity.

Several months after that, another home health aide that came in to help asked one day if she could only work half a day because of something important that was going on in her family. He told me over the telephone that he responded by saying, "Yes, but if you do, you will only be paid for half the day." In saying this, he sounded like Scrooge in the movie *The Christmas Carol* that he claimed to love watching so much and I told him so, but it had no impact in terms of him waking up to how terribly he was behaving.

I then asked him, "Well, how did she react?" He replied, "She said, 'Okay, then I will stay the whole day.'" Obviously, she needed the money and so had to forgo being present to her family as she had wanted.

After I hung up the telephone with my friend, I reflected on what he did as well as what his view was of his actions—even after I challenged him. What I found remarkable was that he didn't seem to feel badly about how he reacted. It made me look at the times I have felt proud about what I have given financially or in other ways when I hadn't responded to what others *truly* needed, rather than simply what I felt like offering them out of my surplus or need for expressing thanks.

I realized that true generosity is rare. At least I know it often is in me and that I often hide that fact from myself. It is a shame when we miss the opportunities to really help because when I examine them in retrospect, I can see that it is not simply the person asking, it is really God requesting my help. My hope is that I can see such Divine callings more readily in the future *and even look for them!*

It may be as simple as the size of a tip left for the housekeeper where you are staying or the way you thank others for the service received in grocery stores or from street vendors.

The opportunities to share of ourselves are innumerable if "only" we have the eyes to see and, of most spiritual importance to ourselves, the right attitude when giving to others.

What we often don't realize is that it is actually quite freeing when we give with a sense of *mitzvah*—giving expecting nothing in return. When we give like this, we don't have to be concerned about gratitude, or even a smile or a positive reaction. God is already smiling at us because we haven't forgotten his other children—our brothers and sisters, no matter what their color, creed, or country of origin. After all, when you are feeling the warmth of God's smile, what else do you really need from others?

||||||||||||||||||||||||||||||||||||||||||||||||||||||||||||||||||||||||||||||||||||||||

32. A Problem of Privilege? Keep Your Life in Perspective

Upon returning from one of my two trips into Cambodia to work with relief workers and their organizations to help them manage stress, I learned that I would have to be careful about my reentry reactions after I returned to the United States. As I look back, I still remember one instance of being in a grocery store behind a woman who was complaining about the choice of lettuce they had available. My sense was, "People are starving around the world and you are complaining when you have so much! Get a life!"

Upon reflection, however, I realized I was really doing the same thing in getting upset about her complaints. While people were managing to eke out a living and survive abuse and tyranny without losing their temper, I was getting crazy over the lack of gratitude of this woman in front of me. I knew better, so, in a sense, I was behaving more poorly than she was.

I also had a similar problem in my clinical practice. In one instance, I would be involved in the debriefing of the Catholic Relief Services personnel evacuated from Rwanda during the bloody genocide. In this role, I would listen to their stories of rape, torture, and killings as they would share them repeatedly as a way of coming to grips with what they had experienced.

To this group I would hand out a sheet of the symptoms of Posttraumatic Stress Disorder (PTSD), so when they would encounter some of them, they would know they weren't crazy—the *situation* was crazy! Later, I would move to my other office in the high-rent district and be confronted with someone upset because his partner wasn't being nice or a teenager was testing the limits at home and think to myself, "You feel that is a problem?! I'll tell you what a real problem is." But then, again upon reflection, I would realize that this was a true problem for these persons at the moment and I needed to respect them. Clearly, I was again having reentry problems, so I would need to keep silent until I could adjust to being in the states again.

Yet, as I think back to these different situations, as well as my more recent experience working with caregivers brought to Beirut from Aleppo, Syria, so I could work with them through an Arabic interpreter, I realize how important it is to ask *myself* when I am upset, "Am I approaching this problem from a position of privilege?" Maintaining perspective and being grateful is hard because we develop "gratefulness tolerance." We keep upping the ante as to under what circumstances we would find a reason to be appreciative. As a result, we miss so much that is around us that we take for granted. Also, our seeking is often silly and unproductive. When we look for *different* and get it, it becomes more of the same. When we look for *more*, and we get it, usually "the more" becomes the norm. If we look for *perfect* in a relationship or possession, even if we think we have attained it, it would possess us (symbiosis), not we it, him, or her. Besides, only God is perfect.

Most of us aren't ungrateful on purpose though. So, what is the answer?

I think it takes a sense of awareness that requires us to be more attentive *on a daily basis* to the simple gifts of life: the ability to take a walk when many can't; the chance to enjoy a meal with friends or have someone serve us in a restaurant, when people around the world are starving; the safety we take for granted when so many are under threat. (In Aleppo, for example, people who needed to drive at night did so without their car lights on so they wouldn't be a target of snipers.)

Complaining is natural for most of us...so we need to make it *unnatural*. It is not that we should stop standing against even little injustices in our midst or allow people or events to hurt us without speaking up. However, by taking a few moments each morning to remember our many gifts and to reflect a few moments each day on how we are blessed, we can gain, maintain, and regain a healthy perspective more easily. When this happens, even when we do protest something, we will not do it out of a sense of being deprived, which will lead to our reaction being out of proportion. Instead, we will do it in a measured way and be more accepting of those who can't and subsequently not let them upset us so easily.

What I notice is that to those who are grateful, more seems to come their way to fulfill them. I think one of the reasons is that grateful persons have the eyes to see all the wonders *already* around them. They can also have more fun with the gifts within their own personality and share them more freely and abundantly with others without expecting anything in return. In their way of thinking, they feel, "Why would I need anything for simply being and sharing who I am? After all, such talents were gifts to me from God in the first place. In addition, there are so many people who have been and still are in my life who have helped me without expecting anything. I should follow their modeling."

So, at the very least, when we are annoyed or upset at something, it might be a good idea to ask ourselves, "Am I approaching this problem from a position of privilege?" It might save a lot of unnecessary aggravation, help us to be more grateful, and in the process become a happier, more psychologically content person.

Moreover, from a spiritual vantage point, gratefulness offers us even more. This is so because when we seek to be grateful, we are more apt to recognize a narrow portal to meet God in new ways that is easy to miss. This is so because when we embrace gratefulness, we can see new ways to join autonomy (our will) with theonomy (God's will). In doing so, we are in a better position to experience life more graciously and become freer to enjoy it. In the process, we begin to demonstrate a deeper faith and have low expectations and high hopes that God will respond to our deep needs.

I think Jesus was right when he said, "To whom much was given, more will be added." He really knew about the gift of gratefulness, and I must admit that this really puzzles me about him. After all, how could he know this? He hadn't taken even a single psychology course!

33. The Pain of a Full Life

One Christmas when I was dressing the tree, I was noticing the homemade ornaments that my daughter and two granddaughters had made when they were children. The experience caused me to smile, laugh, and stop to admire their creativity. It was also a time when I could recall the love for my wife and me that was expressed through these gifts from them.

Then a strange thing happened: Suddenly, I became sad and teared up. I began to realize while these ornaments represented the good relationships I felt I had with them and the fun times we had experienced together, they also brought home to me the key times I had missed spending time with them. Either I had been on the road working with others in a distant place or, as it turned out later in life, my daughter needed to move with her husband to a place that took two planes to reach, so we missed some of the events in our grand-children's lives given my crazy workload.

Sometimes I was very fortunate. Even amid a packed sched-ule, spaces were there to be with them during an important event in their lives and, to be honest, in mine as well. Once, when my young-est granddaughter was in fourth grade, she called and said to me, "Pop-Pop, 'Special Persons Day' is coming up again. They don't have those days after the fourth grade. Can you come?" I could and I still remember proudly sitting there with her.

Another was the confirmation of my oldest granddaughter. The diocese didn't let the parish know when it would happen until about a month before the big day. Finally, it was announced that it would be in October. I had six events in four states in October, but that week-end was free! It gave me a chance to be present and to give her a let-ter I wrote to her as well as a copy of a little book of short reflections I had written many years ago, titled "Snow Falling on Snow." But, because of my chosen work as what might be termed a "Resiliency Psychologist," there were many other times when I would have liked to have been part of the "little" treasured times in their lives, like some of my friends were able to do with their family, but I couldn't.

Another wonderful memory is of flying home from lecturing in New Zealand the week before Christmas. I landed in California, and during the layover, I called home to give them an update on my flight. Instead of my wife answering, my daughter, who just returned home for vacation from university, answered the telephone. You could tell she was happy she received the call and could update her mother.

Hearing the excitement in her voice made the anticipation of spending time together for Christmas even more magical.

As all these thoughts and emotions were washing over me while I was dressing the tree, I recalled a similar message shared by a Methodist military chaplain. While he did truly believe he had responded to the call of God to be with members of the military when they were alone and far from home, in the process he missed so many important events in his family while performing this ministry. This is a sadness I didn't really "get" when he first shared it with me until the same realization dawned on me in a very tangible way in my own life.

Even when the discernment to take a certain path is correct, it doesn't mean there won't be sacrifices for you or those you love. In leading a full life, there is the pain that many around us who don't follow the same path will never know about. It is not that they are not doing enough; it is pure nonsense to think that. They are living a full life in other ways and in turn missing other things that cause them pain. The important thing to recognize though is that in every full life of compassion, true prayer, and commitment, at times there is also present a sense of loss, rejection, failure, and missed opportunities.

Knowing this and being aware that others like myself truly are aware of the pain that comes with trying to do your best hopefully can help. Because when you are aware that you are not alone, you can then see the smile of God through the solidarity with others at the very time when you feel sad and tearful. When that happens, the pain is not removed, but there is an ability to take heart. This comes in the form of space opening up within you to experience the joy and goodness of how you have served and helped people see God anew at a time when they were suffering.

It also helps you to be more in the moment rather than in the silver casket of nostalgia or in the future in your mind doing great things. James Joyce said of one of his characters, "Mr. Duffy lived a short distance from his body." In an awakening prompted by the pain of living a full life, hopefully, we can come home to the present, to those around us now, and to God rather than off in a cognitive cocoon of worry or regret. Reflecting on the pain of a full life by yourself and with others can help in that regard. It is a wake-up call that should be answered with gentleness and clarity rather than avoided, buried, or worse, beating yourself up for not being perfect and everywhere at once.

||||||||||||||||||||||||||||||||||||||||||||||||||||||||||||||||||||||||||||||||||||||||||||||||||||||||

34. Carry Forth the Healthy Heritage and Leave the Rest

When I sit with psychotherapy patients, it is not unusual for them to share dysfunctional elements of their upbringing. In hearing this, while not disagreeing with them, I am careful not to verbally agree with them for fear of causing a problem of *divided loyalty* in which they feel they have betrayed those they love.

This is also reflected in society as a whole. When I was a U.S. Marine Corps officer, we would constantly complain about the Corps. However, if someone in the area from another branch of the military service agreed, we would bristle and ask them, "What do *you* know?!" It was all right for us to say something but not someone outside of the Corps.

The same can be said about those of us who live in the United states or belong to a certain religious denomination or faith tradition. We can make critical comments, but we resist the negative assessments of others outside of the group.

Having said all this, a healthy critique of our own family, country, and faith tradition is essential so we don't carry forth negative aspects of the past. Therefore, first, I will often ask those who want me to walk alongside them, what are the truly good characteristics of their family, society, and religion that they value and want to bring forward in their own lives. Once they have shared these positive elements and can see me appreciating their value, I then ask them what they wish to leave back. With the positive elements in place, they then feel freer to share negative elements without feeling a sense of divided loyalty or that they have betrayed their heritage.

With this in mind, I found the following comments to be of real value. They come from Rudolf Karl Bultmann, a German Lutheran theologian and professor of New Testament at the University of Marburg: "Real loyalty does not involve repetition but carrying things a stage further"; and "Freedom from the past does not result in the denial of the past but in the positive appreciation of it." He also said, "Grace can never be possessed but can only be received afresh again and again."

We must be willing to cast a critical eye on our family, society, and religion, but not do this in disrespect. Instead, we should do it because we love what is good about them and appreciate our responsibility to *carry this heritage a step forward*. No parents are perfect—usually they had something wonderful to offer us but made mistakes as well. No country is perfect—each has a history filled with wonder and sacrifice as well as wrongdoing. No organized religion is perfect—each major religion or denomination has helped so many of their followers to find truth and life in ways not possible without their guidance, yet all religious traditions have stumbled at times.

The call we must respond to today is to carry forth the healthy heritage we have been given...and leave the rest! Otherwise, we will be blindly worshiping the past. Instead, we are called to shoulder the responsibility of ensuring the dynamism of the present and hope for the future of our family, faith tradition, and country. It would be a shame if we set aside this challenge because of fear of change, personal comfort, or an unconscious desire to idolize the past. Moreover, foregoing the joy of experiencing the evolution of our family heritage, the living out of our country's stated values, or the continuous evolution of our faith tradition, is costly in the long run, though it may feel safer to do so in the moment. Think about this the next time you are tempted to defend the status quo rather than entering the temporary alley of darkness in order to discern the necessary change that leads to new light and life in the people, country, and religion you love.

SPIRITUAL FORMATION

35. Conducting Your Own Daily Self-Debriefing

Even when you do "darkness for a living," like I do as someone who works with healers and helpers who are under great stress themselves, I find that it is always dangerous to your psychological and spiritual health if you don't stay alert, humble, and aware.

Years ago, when I was asked to do the psychological and spiritual debriefing of relief workers and their organizations that evacuated from Rwanda after the genocide, I gladly agreed. When I saw each person, I would listen to their repeated stories of the horror they had experienced. They needed to tell their stories just like people in a car accident need to tell their story again and again until they can adjust to what had happened to them that was out of their ordinary experience.

I would then give them a handout on the symptoms of PTSD so they would know *they* weren't crazy—the *situation* was crazy!

After some time, they seemed to get a grip on the situation, and I let my guard down. I thought, "This isn't going so badly." A mistake on my part. Then, someone came in to share an especially tragic story involving children. In response, I could feel myself holding onto the chair for dear life. Even though I had worked in Cambodia twice, something about her sharing was disrupting my sense of self.

Later that day, I did what we call in my business a "counter-transferential review." Quite simply, it is when at the end of a day, the healer or helper first reviews and debriefs the events of the day. They first look at *what* they have encountered (the *objective*) and then the *subjective* (what they *felt and thought* about it all). Most of us do this informally, but my belief is that we need to do this more intentionally, so we don't unduly carry with us the pain and suffering of others into our night and life.

When I did this, I realized that I was holding onto the chair because I was fearful that in being exposed to this person's tragic story, I would be pulled into the vortex of darkness myself. As a result, I not only did a thorough self-debriefing of my feelings, beliefs, and fears but also called a colleague to debrief with him. The result was that I was not simply left with being burdened with nebulous negative feelings and worries. Instead, I now had an opportunity to learn from what I had experienced so I could become more sensitive to what was important and resilient in my work with others.

The "daily self-debriefing" is not just for helpers and healers or when dramatically difficult situations arise. It is for all of us. At the end of a day, when we take a period lasting from several minutes to a more significant period of time to review the day, we can recognize and dispel dysfunctional thinking, empty ourselves of feelings that are draining our positive energy, and teach ourselves to understand what we can control and what we can't so we can "simply" do what we are called to do and let God take care of the residue.

||||||||||||||||||||||||||||||||||||||||||||||||||||||||||||||||||||||||||||||||||||||||

36. Beware the "Tyranny of Hope"

Because my work centers on helping people reach out without being pulled down, others ask, "What is one challenge you notice in working with truly compassionate people?" I don't have to think twice to answer: "They are too hard on themselves and expect too much from others."

One of the reasons for this is what I refer to as the "tyranny of hope." I see it especially in new psychotherapists and relief workers or their organizations when they set goals that seem quite beneficial for their patients or clients. Yet, in such cases, the objectives they set are often much too high for those they are treating or assisting. The result? A burden on the person seeking help and ultimate discouragement for the helper. Without diagnosing a situation and a person, the actions taken while seemingly good can be very misguided.

And so, when parents, professional helpers, politicians, social workers, ministers, educators, or anyone, really, who is filling a role of helping others asks me what to do about the tendency to be discouraged by the resistance they encounter, I offer them these ideas to ponder:

One, first look at what gifts the person has, not simply their needs. This is important no matter how many problems or challenges they are facing because, in the end, it is *their* gifts that will help them to enjoy their lives, to face their challenges, and in turn help them to eventually reach out of themselves to help others.

Two, let them ventilate completely about the problems they see as coming from outside. It is important to do this because most people focus more on that than on themselves. The injustices, real or imagined, must be honored.

Three, have them then uncover what their role might be in making things better or worse. This is not done to blame themselves but instead to become more empowered. Most good done in therapy, coaching, spiritual direction, or mentoring is by focusing in a nonjudgmental way on what the persons themselves can do to impact a situation, even after the fact.

Finally, with a spirit of "positive parallel process," encourage those who come to us to better see the gifts in others and in situations so they can make the most of their surroundings. Very difficult situations sometimes make me smile and think, "I really will need to up my game now so I can see what it is possible for me to actually do and also receive from this situation in the process of my reaching out to others." I suggest we do the same rather than becoming discouraged by the challenges and resistances to our own expectations.

Sometimes, I can see the disapproval in the eyes of a parent of a middle-aged adult child of theirs. It is the same look they had when their adult child was very little. It is like they keep expecting change to take place. Instead, it is important for them to recognize others, including their children, for who they are and what they can do, and then call them to be their best.

Low expectations and high hopes for others allow us to see others' gifts, accept (not simply resign ourselves to) what they can do, and be open to any positive changes that may come about. In this way, rather than a tyranny of hope that is hurtful for all involved, there is a sense of true hope that says I will do what I can and let God take care of the residue. That's faith based on doing what we can and having a prayerful sense of situations and people.

One bishop once said, "I don't know if prayer does any good, but I do notice that when I stop praying, a lot of good things stop happening."

In the morning, some reflective or meditative time spent in silence allows many of my unrealistic demands (even if they seem to be "good ones") to rise to the surface. I see my ego involved. I see my discouragement. Yet I also see that by deflating them and *simply* being present each day to others in the best way possible, while expecting nothing in return and letting God take care of the residue, I have the ticket to compassion in me that resists fading under the stress of my expectations for the results I want.

True prayer also calls us to stop blaming others—including God—for not doing something. I still remember the words of Jack Nelson when he reflected, "As I was walking the streets of Calcutta and saw the poverty surrounding me, I started to scream at God. Then I finally realized that in the suffering of the poor, God was screaming at me."

A distorted sense of hope doesn't help anyone and may even cause harm. Whereas having low expectations and high hopes, doing what we can, and praying as a way to recognize that we are part of a community of others praying and acting as well, we are involving ourselves in a deep act of faith that underlies *true* hope. Not a bad idea, especially during these difficult times.

37. The Garden

A simple, prayerful reminder at the start of the week, nothing more:

I want to walk in the Garden
and have You as a companion,
as my grandfather did before me.

So You can softly encourage
and help me avoid the stones
that trip me when I'm alone.
I need to hear the birds sing
together with Your voice
in the shade of the old trees.

And see Your smile
as the sun touches the flowers
and makes their faces laugh.

Yes, I can't walk alone in the garden.
I need You at my side
just as my grandfather did before me.

Robert J. Wicks, *Snow Falling on Snow*
(Mahwah, NJ: Paulist Press, 2001)

38. Lean Back Now…So You Don't Need to Step Back Later

Several years ago, at the height of two wars in the Middle East, I was at Walter Reed Army Hospital to speak to the physicians, psychologists, and nurses about their own *secondary* stress (pressures experienced in reaching out to others). At the break, one of the physicians said to me that he felt his "life and marriage was going down the tubes." I asked him to put me in the picture.

He responded by saying that he had recently returned from a deployment in the Middle East and was sure he was going back again soon. While at Walter Reed all he did was cut people's legs off. In his own words, "I'd like to take a damn gall bladder out for a change." Then he would go home and try to calm down by going upstairs and hitting golf balls into a cup. When he did this last time, his wife burst into the room and said, "You spend most of your time at work, then you come home and hit golf balls rather than being with me and the boys. This family is going nowhere!"

After a few seconds of quiet to let his emotions settle, I asked, "Well, what do you do immediately after work?" He stared incredulously at me and said in a gruff voice, "Why, go home of course!" He was now angry at me. (This happens a lot to me in my work.)

"Well," I said, "you can't do that." Then I added the following explanation for my remarks: "When you are in a restaurant and go to the bathroom, you see a sign over the sink that says, 'If you work here, you must wash your hands before returning to work.' Well, in the hospital, you must wash your hands not only after you go to the bathroom but *before* you go to the bathroom. Otherwise, you will not only possibly contaminate yourself from your contacts on the floor in the hospital but also run the risk of subsequently contaminating others in the process. The same can be said for us with respect to psychological and spiritual contamination.

"Therefore, after work, take a few moments to walk on the floors or go down to your car and sit there for a while to let the day's dust settle. During this period of 'alone-time' you may be tempted to go down three dark alleyways: *arrogance* (where you project the blame on others), *ignorance* (where you condemn yourself), and *discouragement* (where you expect things to change immediately). Instead, sit in the quiet with a spirit of *intrigue* and let the days feelings and thoughts move through you like a train. Don't entertain them or suppress them but quietly let yourself know that you have done what was humanly possible today given who you are. End these few quiet moments with the mantra: *I will do what I can again tomorrow by releasing and learning from what has happened today.* This time spent allowing the 'dust of the day' to settle before rejoining the family is analogous to 'washing one's hands' in order to cleanse the mind and heart of the detritus of the day."

When we lean back like this, it gives us the chance to reflect, reappraise, and renew. This helps to keep us in a psychologically resilient place to reach out to others in worse shape than we are. When we don't do it, stress can quietly slip up on us. Marshall McLuhan once said, "If the temperature of the bath rises one degree every ten minutes, how will the bather know when to scream?" Those of us who have as a significant part of our role reaching out to others—and who among us doesn't—often don't know when to scream today. As a result, many of us may not be burning out, but we are having a "brown out" and losing some of the joy of being alive and being an encouraging presence for others.

Taking a few minutes of silence and solitude each day and wrapping yourself in gratitude cannot only prevent this from happening but also can help us to gain, maintain, and regain a healthy perspective. Not a bad deal for taking a few minutes with the right spirit before the day begins and after the activity quiets down. Furthermore, by psychologically and spiritually leaning back in this way, we won't have to step back out of doing the good we do. Instead, we may learn to do it more humbly and appreciate more deeply that good change may take more time than we expect and may come in positive ways that we will never see.

||||||||||||||||||||||||||||||||||||||||||||||||||||||||||||||||||||||||||||||||||||||||||||||||||||||

39. Alone-Time: A Way to Make the Whole World Your Church

Creative writer Anne LaMotte once wrote, "Almost anything will work again if you unplug it for a few minutes...including *you*." Her words came to mind when I was up on Capitol Hill speaking to some Members of Congress and then a larger group of their Chiefs of Staff. I heard that when one Senator was asked, "What is the greatest challenge facing the American Congress today?" he replied, "Not enough time to think."

I believe the same can be said about our spiritual life. The challenge for most of us is that we think that "alone-time" is a luxury. However, without it, we cease to be able to enjoy and share freely the gift of life given to us. "Alone-time," time spent in silence and solitude or simply being quietly reflective even when in a group, provides us with the psychological and spiritual inner space to breathe and "simply" be.

Yet many of us resist such time. This is often so because during those quiet periods, we create a mental vacuum. Because nature abhors a vacuum, often the information in our preconscious, that mental area just below our level of awareness, rises into our consciousness. We can see more clearly the fears, games, worries, anxieties, angers, lack of faith, and desires that are lying just beyond our normal thinking.

People sometimes get upset during quiet moments when this information rises to the surface. However, this should not be so because the only memories that will hurt us are the ones that are present just beyond our awareness and operate as invisible mental puppeteers. Also, if we truly believe in God's love, or need to recognize that we don't at this point, it is important to face *all* our thoughts and beliefs while silently walking with the Lord in the garden of new possibilities.

Therefore, I always encourage people to take at least two minutes each day to sit in silence and solitude while wrapped in gratitude before God. If it helps, I suggest that a person first read a bit of Sacred Scripture or take a word to heart, like *gentleness* or *Mary* or *Jesus*, and use that as a mantra. This frees us from rushing to our grave doing "practical things" while thinking this is the best way to live. I also ask people to walk with God in silence and enjoy the gifts that are around them—the trees in a rural area, the bustling energy of a city—instead of simply walking mindlessly in a cocoon of thought while missing God's gifts and the signs that are present in the ordinary surroundings in which we live.

People will often ask me, "Why only two minutes?" and I respond, "Well, how long are you doing it now?" Just as in the case of physical exercise, regularity is more important than only sporadically doing it for longer periods. Hopefully, these two minutes will expand into more time as we take the following straightforward steps toward enhancing alone-time in our lives:

1. **Give priority to alone-time in your schedule:** To quote Stephen Covey again, "Don't simply prioritize your schedule...schedule your priorities." I have found that taking out time in silence and solitude each morning is the most important way to center myself—especially during busy dark periods.

2. **Use the spaces that are already there:** There are many "crumbs of alone-time" already in your schedule—the quiet moments before you jump out of bed in the morning; when in the shower; during a break in the day; lunchtime; on the drive home; or just before you fall asleep.

3. **Expand the number of places where you can experience alone-time:** Instead of simply thinking you need a special place (church) to be quiet and grateful in front of the Lord, think of times when

you are in traffic, on a line, sitting in a park or your office or at night feeding milk to your child as holy places of alone-time.

4. **Reflect with the right spirit:** Ann LaMotte once quipped, "My mind is like a bad neighborhood....I don't like to go there alone." In other words, make the world your church by always avoiding judging yourself, picking on others, or becoming discouraged. Instead, allow yourself to be *intrigued* even when you feel a negative sense about yourself, others, or the situation.

5. **Just start where you are:** Simply enjoy quietly being with yourself and your environment and appreciate that all is gift. In the quiet, you may see more of the gifts that are around you. There is no need to compare yourself with other meditators or people that pray. Instead, remember Jesus's words in John 15:14—"You are my friends"—and know that life is fleeting. As a sign of gratitude, slow down and see the people around you who soon may be gone. Recall the smiles of those who love you, and appreciate what you are being called to be and do— and then do it! We will then see that prayer during alone-time doesn't pull us away from life. Instead, it renews and enlightens us so that we can be part of good efforts in helpful ways.

Then when someone asks you, "What does alone-time offer you?" you will be able to respond from experience:

- It helps me to be clear, sort things out, and deepen myself.
- It helps me to see more fully both my gifts and foibles.
- It increases my enjoyment in being with myself.
- It provides less dependence on reinforcement by others.

- It enables me to recognize my games, anger, feelings of entitlement, greed, and cowardice.
- It protects my inner fire.
- It helps me to accept change and loss—everyone needs time to adjust to change and grieve losses.
- It helps me to recognize my compulsions in life—the mental noise that comes to mind as I reflect.
- It lets me spend time alone with God rather than with my own ego and to listen to the Spirit rather than simply to my own desires.

Alone-time in the presence of God is the portal to a healthy perspective. It makes the whole world a church, whereas, without it, the only time you will see what is really important is when someone is ill or dying or another tragedy befalls you. It is a shame to live like that when it is unnecessary and a waste of life...your *own* life.

40. Two Questions for You

Many years ago, minimalist poet Robert Lax asked his friend and writer Thomas Merton shortly after he was baptized, "What do you want to be?" He responded that he wanted to be a good Catholic. Lax retorted that he should say he wanted to be a saint. Merton was surprised by this and said that this was impossible and asked how he could ever be a saint. Lax responded that if Merton simply had the desire, God would give him the grace to become one.

But do we really want to be a saint? The commitment to be one takes a willingness to release, to *let go*.

A priest I know, when he was visiting a class in an elementary school, asked some children, "Who wants to be a saint? In response, all but one little girl raised their hands.

The priest asked her why she didn't raise her hand.

"Because I don't want to die yet," she replied. At this point, the priest said that the rest of the class put down their hands.

Yet, with true prayer we do raise our hands, we seek to be saints, we say we are willing to die—not by physically dying but through *kenosis*, an emptying, a dying to what is unnecessarily filling and preventing us from seeing, from *experiencing*, God and life in new more relevant ways. This many not simply be things, but could be beliefs, ways of dealing with life at the stage of life we are in now, or something that we are demanding as a price for being happy.

One theologian once said that "Jesus didn't call us to a new religion but to *life*." This is the type of attitude we need when we pray. An attitude based on a good relationship with God and a willingness to be open to see beyond our little world.

Given this, I would like to pose two interrelated questions. The first is an obvious one for those who wish to be open to receive new life each day. It is based on Jesus's simple, direct, challenging statement: Where your treasure is, your heart is. The question is, What do you need to die to at this point in order to become free?

The second is one that was presented to me by a Marist Brother at an important turning point in my life: What do you know about God that you didn't learn from a book?

41. Finding the Right Mentor

"When you see a good person, think of becoming like her or him. When you see someone not so good, reflect on your own weak points."

—Confucius

Years ago, I was sitting with a good friend who was a psychologist. He was telling me about an article he had read in *The New Yorker* magazine about a person whose therapist had died on him. Suddenly, he stopped and filled up with tears. I asked him, "What's the matter?" He waited a moment to regain his composure. Then he said, "You know, Bob, I have been in therapy and I have had clinical supervision, but I never had a mentor, and it is something I sorely missed in my life." As I sat there listening to him, his words reminded me of the time when Swiss psychiatrist Carl Jung posed this question: "Where are the wise and wonderful persons of old who do not merely talk about life but live it?"

People from many diverse backgrounds testify to the impact of having a good mentor. For example, Buddhist Matthieu Ricard, in his widely read book *Happiness* wrote, "Everything changed when I met a few remarkable beings who exemplified what a fulfilling life can be." Steve Georgiou, in his delightful work *Way of the Dreamcatcher*, wrote about minimalist poet Robert Lax (who was also the best friend of Trappist monk and spiritual writer Thomas Merton): "I remember how after spending long evenings with Lax, I would leave his hermitage and feel as if I had landed on the earth for the first time." I personally remember meeting for a single visit with someone whom I felt was a sage and thought to myself afterward, "I don't think I aged in his presence. Aging takes friction and this man was totally nondefensive." When I finally did find a mentor (Flavian Burns, Thomas Merton's final abbot), I was able to walk through much of my life's wishes, blocks, thoughts, and hopes with someone who truly was able to accept and gently guide me.

Andrew Harvey, in his classic spiritual work *Journey in Ladakh*, shared with a traveling companion that it is hard to believe that there was anyone who could help him. To which his companion responded simply, "That is because you have not found such a person yet."

So, in the search, what traits do we look for when we are seeking a mentor? Although I think finding all the traits or gifts you wish in one person might not be possible, I did include a list in my book *Night Call: Embracing Compassion and Hope in a Troubled World* indicating that my ideal mentor would have an ability to

- Ask questions that invigorate my thinking to see both possibility and challenge in new ways
- Help me to return to the clatter and commotion of my life a little differently with a way of living with humility and dignity in this transient, anxious world
- Not ask me to have faith in him or her but demonstrate a faith in me
- Be in touch with a truth that seemed bigger than the truths I was living by
- Be as sincere as I hoped I was

- Recognize that I was looking for some meaning, peace, and joy as well as to understand myself a bit better than all my training and experience had offered me up to this point
- Help me to see more clearly that the mentoring process isn't simply my listening to a mentor so carefully that I would know everything the mentor did but instead through listening with a sense of true openness I might find a way to mature what I already have within me
- Offer me the "psychological room" to be myself
- Encourage a sense of wonder and awe in me about being who I am now and who I can be as I turn the corners of different phases in my life and work
- Stand with me in the darkness until I find a new perspective and deeper sense of self that might not have been possible had the difficulties not appeared in the first place.
- Be practical and mindful of the realities of life but not captured by them
- Share his or her *charism* (gift) or primary psychological signature strength in a way that might allow me to find and fathom mine more deeply than before
- Provide guidance without giving answers; offer support but not remove my own independence and faith in myself to discover an approach that would be most suitable given my own personality and circumstances

Both receiving and offering mentoring is a gifted event. It is not magic. We still need to decide what is best and then act on this knowledge ourselves, but the relationship with a mentor is one that can make all the difference in how we proceed in life. Now, finding the right one, although not as impossible as some would think, is still another matter.

‖‖

42. Perspective: The Key to Wisdom, Resilience, and Compassion

In the end, it is not the amount of darkness in the world, your country, religion, family, or even yourself that matters. It is how you stand in that darkness that makes the difference. It is your *perspective*, the way you see things, that is key to whether the obstacles and different views encountered will help you to deepen as a person and soften your soul or simply make you bitter and rigid.

Although psychology and psychiatry have known for years about the value of possessing a healthy perspective, religion and classic philosophy have embraced this wisdom for even longer.

In the Talmud, we sense this message: You do not see things as they are; you see things as *you* are.

In the New Testament, we feel the power of the following words of Jesus, "If your eye is healthy, your whole body will be full of light" (Matt 6:22).

In Buddist Classical Writings, it is the unobstructed vision.

In the Upanishads, Hindus see it as a turning-around in one's seat of consciousness.

We can even sense "perspective" behind the words of spiritual leaders throughout the centuries. The prophet Muhammad, for example, purportedly said, "If you have enough money to buy two loaves of bread, by only one, and spend the rest on flowers."

A healthy perspective is at the heart of resilience, happiness, and compassion. At its center is a willingness to be humble enough to be open to see life differently when needed so you can resist prejudice and deepen as well as broaden your outlook. This should not be surprising, because when you take knowledge and add humility, you get wisdom. When you take that wisdom and add it to compassion, you get love, and love is at the center of a meaningful, rewarding, and compassionate life. God is love, and *all* of us are his children. No exceptions.

43. To Competent, Caring Persons: How Are *You* Doing?

Several years ago, I met a former student who is very talented, compassionate, and committed to an array of wonderful causes. When I asked her how she was doing, she stopped smiling, seemed to fill up with tears, and after a pause said in a quiet voice, "No one has asked me that in a *long* while. I am always the one asking that question."

Competent caring people are usually surrounded by others who turn to them for solace, support, and concern about their own welfare. When someone found out that my main role was working with others experiencing *secondary* stress (the pressures experienced in reaching out to others), he asked me who helped me with my "tertiary" stress. Since I was there for other helpers, he wanted to know who was there for me. Certainly, it was a fair and insightful question, and I answered him as to what I did for myself so I could continue living as meaningful and rich a life as possible.

Even though I am careful to ensure self-support, after a long series of travels, I can sense that my "soul is tired" at times, that I need a break, and to receive the interest of others in my welfare. The challenge for us who support others though is that we project a sense of competence and strength, through the resilience and joy in our lives. While this projection reflects reality for most of the time, there are occasions when there is a need for all of us to have some extra quiet renewing time as well as others there to support and encourage us when we are feeling especially vulnerable. The problem is that those of us who are in helping and healing roles—as parents, professional clinicians, teachers, or mentors—are usually not viewed as people in need. The pressures continue to be piled on by others without a sense that our psychological and spiritual arms may be getting weaker and weaker.

Therefore, it is important for competent caring persons to have those in their life who will ask, "How are *you* doing?" In addition, there is a need to be aware of developing renewing elements in our own life that will give new energy and help engender a different, deeper perspective when it is temporarily lost. Also, a good aid is knowing what signs trigger the need for us to reach out and within for new sources of resilience. Some of them might be the following:

- A feeling of tearfulness at encountering a small, sad event that normally wouldn't cause such a strong reaction
- Feelings of anomie or alienation even when surrounded by a group of people who are doing good things and mean well
- Daydreaming of a beautiful place you wish you were visiting at this point rather than being where you are
- Questions about your own positive impact on others even when there is plenty of evidence that you *actually are* doing some really nice things
- A sense of "lostness" at a point in your life
- Being ill-tempered or sarcastic when such a response is not the usual one for you
- Having an unusually negative reaction to persons wanting to share what is going on in their lives but are seemingly uninterested in what is happening in yours—even when they do this all the time and you normally simply laugh it off
- Experiencing a strong sense of gratitude for a small gesture of kindness by someone you don't know

In reference to that last trigger, I once had this reaction on Veteran's Day while in a store. The clerk found out I had been a Marine Corps officer and said, "Oh, you not only get a discount today, but we would also like to give you five free cookies from a batch we just baked." When I heard this, I felt as if someone had just given me the greatest gift ever and felt deeply thankful for their consideration of my service. In dramatically reacting this way, I knew I was psychologically and spiritually on empty. So, I want to say to all of you as competent, caring persons, what people sometimes say only to military veterans today:

Thank *you* for *your* service.
And, the question I want to ask you is,
How are *you* doing?

Your caring means a great deal to others, so please be especially kind to yourself when you need it and find those who will recognize your vulnerability and stand with you in that moment. Also, once again, I want to say to you, *Thank you for your service* and remember that I have said those words to you the next time your soul is tired.

44. Different Types of Gifts I Should Give to Others

Recently, I saw a photograph of a high churchman dressed in all his regalia, including white gloves, sitting on a throne with a gruff look on his face. He is one of the persons who says unflattering words about Pope Francis, whom I find to be a loving servant-leader, whom I admire for his humility. Seeing this, it reminded me that I must seek new ways to give the gift of love to others—even those, *especially* those, with whom I disagree.

I also read some sarcastic comments about those young people who were seeking asylum in the United States. It made me think about how often I have not thought about how my words would hurt others, particularly those whose plight I didn't fully understand. People go through many terrible experiences that I will never know anything about. Knowing this, I need to offer the gift of kindness in everyday life through my words and actions. I need to reflect more about the potential impact before I say, post, or do something.

Also, as I look around in my townhome during Christmas time and see the beautifully dressed tree that was cut down recently, the creche with straw underneath the manager scene, and little lit houses on the top of the bookshelves, I know I should be grateful. However, that gratitude should show itself in giving more financially and more deeply personally to those in need. When someone is speaking to me, for example, it is not enough for me to remain silent waiting for my opportunity to speak. Instead, my silence should be a time for me to truly listen in order to understand the concern of others more deeply before I say or do something.

But all these "gifts" that I need to offer must be based on a greater faith that shows results. After all, of what importance are faith, spirituality, prayer, and a sense of community if they don't help me to

- Be more compassionate and understanding—even with very difficult people—so I don't unhelpfully respond to nastiness with more nastiness;
- Secure a better sense of awareness and responsiveness every day to God's gifts *within* and around me so I feel less needy and more giving;
- Achieve a greater interest in letting go of what is holding me back from being faithful and possessing inner peace through a willingness to launch out onto the infinite pathway of spiritual mindfulness;
- Be more able to soften my soul—and become deeper as a person—when I encounter the pain everyone must experience at different points in life; and
- Experience God as clearly as the problems and joys I face each day?

Yes, I have a lot of gifts in my "spiritual sleigh" that need to be given out around the world not only during Christmastime, but during the rest of the year as well. What an amazing trip it should be. If you would like, hop on board. Your company is most welcome.

‖‖

45. A Modern Lament

Find Me Again, Lord
In the past, there are so many times You have found me, Lord
that I can't even recall all of them anymore.
One moment, I'd find myself feeling all alone
and, the next, You would be at my side.

But now I need You to find me again, Lord.

Let me know You are there
in the splash of a goose landing in the water,

in the noise of a city at night,
or in the quiet of a still forest.

I need you to find me again, Lord.

Help me know you are thinking of me
in the way someone offers a smile,
in the care expressed in a note sent to me,
or simply in a cup of coffee, slowly enjoyed.

I need you to find me again, Lord.

Possibly the tears quietly sitting on my cheek
will remind You once again of me.
Maybe the giggles of a child or broad grin of an old friend
will have me recall Your presence once more.

But whatever it might be,
I need you to find me again, Lord,
so I hope you will whisper my name in some way
so I can feel your intimate presence in my life.

Yes, I need you to find me again, Lord...*soon*.

Note: This reflection may be reproduced and distributed without requesting permission if you include the source: Wicks, Robert J. *Heartstorming: Creating a Place God Can Call Home* (Mahwah, NJ: Paulist Press, 2020).

PART III

Creating Your Own Field Notes

EXPLORING A LIFE OF MEANING, REFLECTION, COMPASSION, AND PRAYER

In the previous chapters, you have had a chance to look at some of my field notes on the spiritual life. In other words, these are reflections I have had on portals to experiencing God in new ways based on interactions, readings, reflections, and prayer. My hope is that they have in some way urged you to open the doors to seeing new possibilities in encountering God in real, concrete ways in your own life by preparing your own field notes.

The following practice of creating your own field notes is a quite simple, constant one. To discover the presence of God in your life and the calling that results from such encounters, there is a need to look back carefully, to learn new ways of being truly present, and to discern future directions we believe we are being asked to take.

LOOKING BACK

At the end of the day, we need only take a few moments alone for a spiritual and theological reflection. This involves the following sequence:

1. Look at the objective peaks, valleys, and routine encounters of the day. This includes bringing to

mind the persons involved, what happened, and any other details about the situation that might be important.

2. It is, then, good to examine the emotions these events and encounters produced. (Please note: You may be surprised that "little" events can produce such profound reactions in some cases.)

3. Once emotions surface, look at the ways of your thinking, perceiving, and understanding that led to such reactions. (Each person may react differently to a single event. What may upset me, you may simply shrug off as unimportant.)

4. Given what the above steps uncovered, decide what conclusions and learnings you can come to regarding what you have learned from this analysis. In addition, from this newly gained knowledge, also ask yourself what actions you think God is calling you to take given this understanding. Finally, in line with this information now grasped, how do you believe your values have been clarified and what choices must you make going forward?

BEING IN THE PRESENT

In one of the movies about the fictional character Harry Potter, his mentor, Albus Dumbledore, says to him, "Harry it's not our abilities that make us who we are; it's our choices."

As we move through the day, we need to be thoughtful, prayerful, remember the spiritual teachings and Sacred Scripture of our faith, as well as sometimes ask other good people for advice before we choose our actions and words.

In our daily life, we are often asked to model what is true and good. As Francis of Assisi aptly noted, "Preach the Gospel always; if necessary, use words." A bit of reflection can keep us in tune with our values and morals, so we can live them out more fully.

DISCERNING FUTURE STEPS AND ATTITUDES

Discernment helps us look at the source of our philosophy, ethic, and behavior. Such an examination helps us see whether the source of a call to live a certain way each day is from God, or if it is primarily due to

- our ego (inordinate self-interest),
- cultural or family pressures,
- a desire to be liked, self-doubt,
- a wish to be successful rather than faithful,
- a fear of not being financially well-off,
- an inordinate need for security, or
- the need to be admired.

Through discernment, we can more clearly see who we are following and for what reason we are acting or believing the way we are. We can also uncover if we are running away from or rejecting outright what in our hearts we have an inkling God is calling us to be and do.

THE REFLECTION PROCESS

Meeting God in any encounter or experience during the day is enhanced when we prepare mental or written spiritual field notes by doing the following:

- Finding time to reflect;
- Selecting meaningful events in our day and life to reflect upon;

- Entering those events by reliving them in our minds;
- Seeking to determine what our emotions and thoughts about them can teach us; and
- Enlivening the knowledge we are given through acting upon what we have learned.

My suggestion is that you engage this process *first* by simply seeking a few moments of alone-time (space by or within yourself). In the following chapter, I am offering questions to use in this quiet space that can open for you new avenues of embracing God in your process of discovery. You can reference them in the categories by which my field notes are also grouped: Priorities, Identity, Openness, Freedom, and Spiritual Formation.

Second, ensure that you put your spiritual and psychological "fingers" on the pulse of your feelings, so you can sense your reaction to what the questions are opening up in you. In doing so, you can simply take note of these reactions or even write them down. Some of your reactions will be quick and strong. Others you may draw a blank on. There are no right or wrong responses. Simply note what comes up for you. Don't criticize yourself or move away from either "negative" or toward "positive" thoughts. Just note them.

There is nothing you need to do about them at this point. No changes are expected of you. Simply be aware and be gentle. You do not need to rush to move on to the next question. Stay with a question for as long as you wish—even a day, a week, or longer. Simply by doing this, you are responding to the call of your heart to move from within according to *kairos* (God's time). Within any category move between questions freely and also move freely between categories, as you sense your needs for discovery. If you only read one question with this spirit of discovery at heart, your pilgrimage will become more evident and richer.

Finally, as you put your trust in God to lead this process, acquaint or reacquaint yourself with Sacred Scripture (a record of discernment between God and us) and be prayerfully open to whatever you learn, whether it is new, familiar, attractive, or unappealing. As Teilhard de Chardin said, "It doesn't matter whether the water is hot or cold if you have to walk through it anyway." So let the journey begin with trust in the Lord and a real sense of intrigue about what God is calling us to see in and around us that would welcome the Spirit in new, more real ways.

Once you have reflected on these heartstorming questions, embracing God and allowing for some quiet space in which to rest and be open, know that you can always return to them again and again if you feel they will help you to move on.

Priorities

1. What preoccupies me during the day, when I am driving or taking a walk, or after I go to bed? (Jesus reminded us, "Where your treasure is, there your heart will be also" [Luke 12:34]. If we are to turn our hearts over to God so we can appreciate the gifts within and around us without being captured by them, an honest search for where our mental energy goes is essential.)

2. How is having a daily recognition of the reality of my mortality (what some refer to as "impermanence") a powerful element in the process of letting go and meeting God in the now?

3. Who models for me a sense of simplicity and an appreciation of awe in their lives, and what is one basic, realistic way that I can follow them, which I can begin practicing now?

4. How can I discern the difference between authentic needs and the ones imposed on me by culture, family, or habit?

5. Why does responding to life's puzzles not require a so-called right answer but one steeped in recognizing the import of the consequence of the choice?

‖‖‖

Identity

1. What would help me find my own voice in light of my identity before God—instead of solely or primarily how the world, my family, and even I may be viewing myself at this time?

2. How do I avoid giving away so much power to the imaginary audiences in my head?

3. What are some of the best ways to uncover and challenge the rumors I have previously believed about myself so I can take greater authorship of the unfolding identity God is calling me to claim?

4. What do I feel remains unlived and unshared in me that God is calling me to remove from under a bushel basket at this point in my life?

5. Why is "unselfconsciousness" such an important goal in becoming the person God is calling me to be?

6. What are ways to discern which family legacies to carry on and which ones I am being called to jettison?

‖‖‖

Openness

1. How can my losses not solely lead to sadness and bitterness but to a depth and a relationship with God that I could never have imagined before?

2. How do I think the letting-go process might involve the unmuting of joy in new areas of my life?

3. What are some of the best catalysts for openness to change and new ways of seeing and making sense of my life and the world (what is often called "meaning-making")?

4. Must I wait until something terrible happens before I let go of a destructive pattern in my life, or can I take an initial, possibly small step in releasing what is preventing me from welcoming God into my heart?

5. What do I feel would be involved in my escaping from a "cognitive cocoon" where I am thinking about you, Lord, so I can experience your presence more fully?

6. What do I need to do in order to see and use my very resistances to change and to seeing the truth as beacons to new personal wisdom about myself rather than merely obstacles to change?

7. What do I need to do now to better receive the graces already around me in life?

8. What should I include in a practical spiritual and psychological "list" of essentials to enhance the processes of letting go, openness, and welcoming God in new ways into my life?

Freedom

1. In what way can I find, and better avail myself of, the "crumbs of alone-time" in my daily schedule, so I can better experience in the silence and solitude a new or different sense of inner freedom each day?

2. What hesitations or fears do I think might be operating that are preventing me from experiencing greater inner freedom in my life at this point?

3. Why is the phrase "expecting nothing in return for what I give to others" such an essential part of the proper spiritual relationship between true compassion and a process of letting go?

4. Where might the spirit of forgiveness come into play with respect to inner freedom?

5. During periods of necessary transition, what is the difference between resignation and acceptance?

6. What is the relationship between "celebrating the temporary" and letting go?

7. What does becoming "a person without guile" have to do with inner freedom?

8. Why does making the most of tradition involve letting go of some past patterns as well?

9. Why is a sense of humor such an integral part of the serious search for inner freedom, being compassionate, and welcoming God?

||||||||||||||||||||||||||||||||||||||||||||||||||||||||||||||||||||||||||||||||||||||||

Spiritual Formation

1. How can I assess the proper roles for criticism and doubt in order to benefit from them?

2. How can I discover and utilize my emotions as a guide to where best I can focus my attention as to what I am holding onto and begin to look at how to let go so I might have more freedom within?

3. In what ways do I think I can improve my ability to achieve greater clarity, even about things I do not wish to see or can't seem to control in my life right now?

4. What are some of the characteristics for me to look for in seeking role models in prayerfulness, compassion, and becoming more of a person without guile for me to emulate?

5. How do I believe, at this point in life, God is asking me to play a more compassionate role?

6. What beneficial, paradoxically positive role do I think asceticism can play in my enjoying life more deeply?

7. What do I need to do to allow spiritual adulthood to become more fully realized in me?

8. When discouragement appears, what are some of the most effective ways I employ to face it?

9. What would be involved in savoring the "spirit of satsang" (the company of good people) at this point in my life?

THE CIRCLE

Warm wishes and blessings on the development of, or continued journaling on, your spiritual field notes—your pilgrimage to create a place for God within yourself and the world.

Lastly, I offer a prayer, "The Circle," from my book *Snow Falling on Snow*:

> Lord, there is so much pain
> in the world.
> Where do I begin to help?
>
> "Start in your circle."
>
> But when I help
> my family and friends
> often they really don't appreciate me.
>
> "But I do."
>
> And when I reach out
> to my coworkers
> some suspect my motives.

CREATING YOUR OWN FIELD NOTES

"I know what is in your heart."

Still, I think I should do more
to help those I don't know
who are suffering in the world.

"Then widen your circle."

But by myself I can't
do much to lighten their great darkness.

"Yes. I know. That is why I am with you."

If only I could believe
You are with me.
If only I could really see you, Lord.

"Open your heart
in prayer
and you will believe and see."

What will I see, Lord?

"That as you walk
through the day
I am the center of your circle."

    Robert J. Wicks, *Snow Falling on Snow*
      (Mahwah, NJ: Paulist Press, 2001)

Appendix

CONTEMPORARY SOURCES AND INSPIRATION

Authors and Books to Consider

Brother Lawrence of the Resurrection, *The Practice of the Presence of God*
Byrd, William, *Alone*
Chadwick, David, *Crooked Cucumber: The Life and Zen Teachings of Shunryu Suzuki*
Demello, Anthony, *One Minute Wisdom*
Dillard, Annie, *The Writing Life*
Du Boulay, Shirley, *Beyond the Darkness*
Elie, Paul, *The Life You Save May Be Your Own*
Ellsberg, Robert, *The Saints' Guide to Happiness*
France, Peter, *Hermits*
————, *A Place of Healing: Patmos*
Frankl, Viktor, *Man's Search for Inner Meaning*
George, Nina, *The Little Paris Bookshop: A Novel*
Georgiou, Steve, *The Way of the Dreamcatcher: Spirit Lessons with Robert Lax*
Griffiths, Bede, *The Golden String*

Grumbach, Doris, *Fifty Days of Solitude*
Harford, James, *Merton and Friends*
Harvey, Andrew, *Journey in Ladakh*
Hershey, Terry, *The Power of Pause*
Heschel, Abraham Joshua, *The Wisdom of Heschel*
Housden, Roger, *Ten Poems to Change Your Life*
Iyer, Pico, *The Open Road*
Maitland, Sara, *A Book of Silence*
Markides, Kyriacos, *Gifts of the Desert*
Matthew, Iain, *The Impact of God*
McGregor, Michael N., *Pure Act: The Uncommon Life of Robert Lax*
Merton, Thomas, *New Seeds of Contemplation*
————, *A Vow of Conversation*
————, *Wisdom of the Desert*
Norris, Kathleen, *Dakota*
Nouwen, Henri, *Genesee Diary*
————, *Making All Things New*
————, *Reaching Out*
————, *Way of the Heart*
Palmer, Parker, *Let Your Life Speak*
Ricard, Matthieu, *Happiness*
Rilke, Maria Ranier, *Letters to a Young Poet*
Ritter, Christiane, *A Woman in the Polar Night*
Rupp, Joyce, *Boundless Compassion*
————, *Praying Your Goodbyes*
(de) Saint-Exupery, Antoine, *A Guide for Grown-ups*
Simmons, Philip, *Learning to Fall*
Steindl-Rast, David, *Gratefulness, the Heart of Prayer*
Storr, Anthony, *Solitude: A Return to Self*
Telushkin, Joseph, *Rebbe*
Tutu, Desmond, with the Dalai Lama, *The Book of Joy*
Wicks, Robert, *After 50*
————, *Everyday Simplicity*

————, *Night Call: Embracing Compassion and Hope in a Troubled World*

————, *No Problem*

————, *Perspective: The Calm within the Storm*

————, *Prayerfulness*

————, *Seeds of Sensitivity*

————, *Simple Changes*

————, *Snow Falling on Snow*

Wicks, Robert (ed.), *Prayer in the Catholic Tradition*

ABOUT THE AUTHOR

For more than thirty-five years, Dr. Robert Wicks, has answered a call to speak calm into chaos for individuals and groups experiencing great stress, anxiety, and confusion. Dr. Wicks received his doctorate in psychology (Psy.D.) from Hahnemann Medical College and Hospital in Philadelphia. He is professor emeritus at Loyola University Maryland and has taught in universities and professional schools of psychology, medicine, nursing, theology, education, and social work. In 2003, Dr. Wicks was the commencement speaker for Wright State School of Medicine in Dayton, Ohio. In 2005, he was both visiting scholar and the commencement speaker at Stritch School of Medicine in Chicago. He was also commencement speaker at Georgian Court University in Lakewood, New Jersey, and Caldwell University in Caldwell, New Jersey, as well as a recipient of honorary doctorates from both.

In the past, Dr. Wicks has spoken on Capitol Hill to members of Congress and their chiefs of staff, and at Johns Hopkins School of Medicine, the U.S. Air Force Academy, the Mayo Clinic, and the North American Aerospace Defense command. Additionally, he has spoken at Harvard's Children's Hospital, Harvard Divinity School, Yale School of Nursing, Princeton Theological Seminary, and the Defense Intelligence Agency, and to members of the NATO Intelligence Fusion Center in England. His major areas of expertise are resilience, self-care, prevention of *secondary* stress (pressures encountered in reaching out to others), and approaches to strengthening spiritual life.

Dr. Wicks has also spoken at the Boston Public Library's commemoration of the Boston Marathon bombing, addressed ten thousand Catholic educators in the Air Canada Arena in Toronto, was the opening keynote speaker to fifteen hundred physicians for the American Medical Directors Association, has spoken at the FBI Academy, led a weeklong course in Beirut for Catholic relief workers from Aleppo, Syria, and addressed caregivers in Beijing, Hanoi, Haiti, India, Thailand, Northern Ireland, Scotland, Hungary, Guatemala, Malta, New Zealand, Australia, France, England, and South Africa.

In 1993, and again in 2001, Dr. Wicks worked in Cambodia. During these visits, he worked with professionals from the English-speaking community who were present to help the Khmer people rebuild their nation following years of terror and torture. In 1994, he was responsible for psychologically debriefing relief workers evacuated from Rwanda during that country's bloody genocide. In 2006, he also delivered presentations on self-care at the National Naval Medical Center and Walter Reed National Military Medical Center, both in Bethesda, Maryland, to those healthcare professionals responsible for Iraqi and Afghani war veterans evacuated to the United States with multiple amputations and severe head injuries. More recently, Dr. Wicks addressed U.S. Army healthcare professionals returning from Africa where they were assisting during the Ebola crisis.

Dr. Wicks has published more than fifty books for both professionals and the general public. He has published several works on spirituality, including *Riding the Dragon*, *Everyday Simplicity*, and *Prayerfulness*. His latest psychological works are *The Tao of Ordinariness: Humility and Simplicity in a Narcissistic Age*, *Night Call: Embracing Compassion and Hope in a Trouble World*, *Perspective: The Calm within the Storm*, and *Bounce: Leading a Resilient Life*. His books have been translated into Chinese, Polish, Indonesian, Korean, and Spanish.

In 2006, Dr. Wicks received the first annual Alumni Award for Excellence in Professional Psychology from Widener University. He is also the recipient of the Humanitarian of the Year Award from the American Counseling Association's Division on Spirituality, Ethics and Religious Values in Counseling. For his service to the Church, he received the papal medal *Pro Ecclesia et Pontifice* from John Paul II.

ALSO AVAILABLE FROM PAULIST PRESS BY ROBERT J. WICKS

After 50

Clinical Handbook of Pastoral Counseling,
Volumes 1, 2, and 3

Handbook of Spirituality for Ministers,
Volumes 1 and 2

Living a Gentle Passionate Life

Living Simply in an Anxious World

Snow Falling on Snow

ADVANCED REVIEWS FOR *HEARTSTORMING*

In *Heartstorming: Creating a Place God Can Call Home*, Robert Wicks offers us a spiritual tonic that invites us to deeply experience God in prayer, within ourselves, in community, and in the simple interactions of everyday life. As well as touching on the topics of "letting go" and encountering God in the "gray periods" of our life ("My Soul Is Tired"), Wicks also provides forty-five brief "field notes" to enrich the spiritual life of even the busiest among us.

Richard Rohr, OFM
Founder, Center for Contemplation
Author, *The Cosmic Christ*

Amid the anxieties of our era, a treasure such as *Heartstorming* comes along to strengthen and enliven the soul. Moving through Robert Wicks's book is like traveling on a river of gold. Each page enriches the reader's spirituality and leads homeward to the heart of the Divine.

Joyce Rupp, OSM
Author, *Boundless Compassion*

PRAISE FOR RELATED BOOKS BY ROBERT J. WICKS

Riding the Dragon (Sorin Books, 2003)

Like a good friend's support in tough times, *Riding the Dragon* is compassionate and wise.

Jack Kornfield, author of *A Path with Heart*

Crossing the Desert: Learning to Let Go, See Clearly and Live Simply (Sorin Books, 2008)

Wonderfully sane, balanced, accessible, witty, and challenging.

Ronald Rolheiser, author of *The Holy Longing*

Bounce: Living the Resilient Life (Oxford University Press, 2009)

Insightful, practical, and often humorous, *Bounce* is the right tonic for the spirit we need in a stressful world.
Helen Prejean, author of *Dead Man Walking*

Perspective: The Calm within the Storm (Oxford University Press, 2014)

This is the kind of book you can't put down because it is so necessary.
Alexandra Fuller, *The New York Times* bestselling author of *Cocktail Hour under the Tree of Forgetfulness*

Night Call: Embracing Compassion and Hope in a Troubled World (Oxford University Press, 2017)

Wicks shows how persistence, compassion, and humility heal us all. His book is a great salve.
Robert F. Kennedy, Jr.